I0473947

U.S. Department of Justice
Office of Justice Programs
810 Seventh Street NW.
Washington, DC 20531

Eric H. Holder, Jr.
Attorney General

Laurie O. Robinson
Assistant Attorney General

Joye E. Frost
Acting Director, Office for Victims of Crime

Office of Justice Programs
Innovation • Partnerships • Safer Communities
www.ojp.usdoj.gov

Office for Victims of Crime
www.ovc.gov

NCJ 235121

October 2011

FOREWORD

Our core mission is to pursue justice for criminal acts, and that pursuit includes justice for the victims of and witnesses to crime. Every day, Department personnel encounter individuals harmed by crime or who witnessed others being harmed by crime. How we treat those individuals has a huge impact on their confidence in the criminal justice system and their ability to heal and recover from crime. When the Department is successful in identifying and convicting offenders, our victim assistance efforts help victims navigate an unfamiliar system, foster accountability, and find affirmation for their suffering. In situations where the Department is unable to identify a perpetrator or bring a perpetrator to justice, our outreach and assistance can help victims access the services they need to recover and help them understand the criminal justice response.

For several decades, crime victims' laws have mandated that Department personnel provide victims with services and make our best efforts to see that victims are accorded their rights. To satisfy our statutory responsibilities, it is essential that Department personnel understand the legal mandates regarding victims and receive clear guidance about how to carry out those responsibilities. This updated edition of the *Attorney General Guidelines for Victim and Witness Assistance* reflects current statutory provisions, recognizes the technological and legal changes that have taken place since the previous Guidelines were promulgated, and incorporates best practices that will benefit victims and enhance investigations and prosecutions. It is my hope that this tool will enhance our ability to vindicate victims' rights and to provide victims with the services that they deserve.

Eric H. Holder, Jr.
Attorney General of the United States

[page intentionally left blank]

CONTENTS

ARTICLE I

GENERAL CONSIDERATIONS

A. Statement of Purpose

The purpose of this document, the *Attorney General Guidelines for Victim and Witness Assistance* (AG Guidelines), is to establish guidelines to be followed by officers and employees of the U.S. Department of Justice (Department) investigative, prosecutorial, correctional, and parole components in the treatment of victims of and witnesses to crime. In 1982, Congress directed the Attorney General to promulgate the first AG Guidelines, which have been revised periodically to reflect changes in the law. (*See* 18 U.S.C. § 1512 note (1984) (Federal Guidelines for Treatment of Crime Victims and Witnesses in the Criminal Justice System)).

These AG Guidelines supersede the *Attorney General Guidelines for Victim and Witness Assistance* (2005 ed.).

B. How To Apply These Guidelines

1. Underlying Authorities

   Federal victims' services and rights laws are the foundation for the AG Guidelines. The core statutes are the Victims' Rights and Restitution Act (VRRA), 42 U.S.C. § 10607 (2006) (containing mandatory services), and the Crime Victims' Rights Act (CVRA), 18 U.S.C. § 3771 (2006 & Supp. III 2009) (containing court enforceable rights), but additional rights and requirements exist in other statutes and rules of criminal procedure. In the text of the AG Guidelines, all statutory requirements or rules of criminal procedure are followed by a direct citation to the applicable statute or rule. Guidelines that are purely Department policy, as opposed to statutory law, will not be followed by a citation. Guidelines that are policy intended to implement a statutory right, provision, or procedural rule will be followed by a citation referring to the statute or rule.

2. Obligation Definitions

   The AG Guidelines use the word "shall" where "shall" appears in a statute or when the policy is mandatory. The use of the term "shall" means that the relevant guideline is mandatory, though room may remain for individual judgment in determining how best to comply with the guideline. When the AG Guidelines use the word "should," personnel are expected to take the action or provide the service described unless there is an appropriate, articulable reason not to do so. When the AG Guidelines use the word "may," personnel are permitted to use their discretion about whether and how to provide assistance. Other language may be used in the AG Guidelines to describe the obligations of personnel; phrases such as "are encouraged" or "make reasonable efforts" are intended to have their usual and customary meaning.

3. Coverage

The AG Guidelines apply to all personnel in the Department who are engaged in or support investigative, prosecutorial, correctional, or parole functions within the criminal justice system. They apply to staff regardless of title, grade, or job description who have contact with victims or take actions that impact victims. Department managers should require all contractors whose employees come into contact with crime victims to provide employee training on AG Guidelines compliance. Department components should encourage non-Department personnel specially assigned or deputized to work with Department components to learn and comply with federal victims' services and rights laws and the AG Guidelines.

The AG Guidelines are intended to serve as a model for guidelines on the fair treatment of crime victims and witnesses for other state and federal law enforcement agencies.

4. Organization

The AG Guidelines are organized around the two primary crime victims' services and rights laws. Articles I and II deal with general policies affecting all components and victims. Article III contains the basic definitions of victim under both of the key laws, as well as sections on unique victim populations. Article IV covers the Department's mandatory obligations to provide services to victims of a crime under the VRRA. Article V covers the CVRA provisions that victims of a charged offense can enforce during a prosecution. Article VI addresses witnesses only. Article VII consists of the Department's statement on non-litigability.

ARTICLE II

GUIDELINES APPLICABLE TO ALL COMPONENTS

A. Encouragement To Provide Services and Assistance

A strong presumption exists in favor of providing, rather than withholding, assistance and services to victims of crime. Federal statutes define mandatory services and court-enforceable rights for federal crime victims that establish a minimum baseline for the Department's obligation to crime victims. Department personnel are encouraged to provide additional assistance to crime victims where appropriate and within available resources, as situations warrant.

B. Victim Declinations of Services and Exercise of Rights

Department personnel are required by law and under the AG Guidelines to identify victims of a crime, notify them of their rights, and offer them services as described in the AG Guidelines. Victims, however, are not required to exercise their rights or to accept these services and may choose at any point in the criminal justice process to decline to receive further services or exercise their rights. Department personnel need not provide services or support the exercise of rights that victims have made an informed decision to decline. When a victim declines to receive services or to exercise rights, Department personnel should attempt to ascertain whether the victim wants to decline all future services and the exercise of all rights or only one or more specific service or right. In the latter case, Department personnel should continue to provide services and support the exercise of rights that have not been declined. The employee should consider documenting the victim's informed declination of mandatory services and the exercise of rights.

C. Privacy and Confidentiality Considerations for Victims and Witnesses

1. Private Information

   Department personnel engaged in the investigation or prosecution of a crime shall be mindful of the privacy concerns of victims and witnesses. In particular, Department personnel should use their best efforts to protect private information by redacting this information from records or documents that will be placed in the public record, unless specifically required by court rules or procedure. (*See, e.g.,* Fed. R. Crim. P. 49.1). Private information includes Social Security numbers, bank account information, dates of birth, and, in some circumstances, may include an individual's identity, address, contact information, or location.

   Department personnel should seek protective orders or employ other means when necessary to safeguard private information from becoming public or from being used in proceedings if the information is not relevant. If private information must be disclosed in proceedings or in the course of discovery, Department personnel should seek protective orders to prevent dissemination of this information outside of the proceedings. (*See also* Fed. R. Crim. P. 17(c)(3)).

2. Sharing of Information for Law Enforcement Purposes

    Although private information should be safeguarded from public disclosure, when necessary, information may be shared among investigative, prosecutorial, corrections, and parole agencies, and with the court or defense. Department personnel directly involved with providing victim and witness assistance should therefore inform victims and witnesses that private information will likely be shared among Department components or may be shared with other law enforcement entities as appropriate, may be shared with the court, or may have to be provided to the defense during the course of discovery. If the victim or witness raises concerns regarding the disclosure of such information that are warranted, Department personnel should employ their best efforts to protect this information from disclosure, or if such a disclosure is required, employ their best efforts to address appropriate and necessary concerns for victims and witnesses.

3. Dissemination of Private Information to the Media or Public

    Department personnel should use their best efforts to refrain from releasing personal or confidential information about victims and witnesses to the press or public. Personal or confidential information in this context may include the individual's name, address, contact information, identifying information, or other information or material that may allude to the identity of the victim or witness. Moreover, Department personnel should refrain from making any public statements that concern the identity, testimony, or credibility of any prospective witness. (Release of Information by Personnel of the Department of Justice Relating to Criminal and Civil Proceedings, 28 C.F.R. § 50.2(b)(6)(iv) (2010)).

    In addition, Department personnel receiving requests for information about a case or matter should be mindful that information generally subject to release under the Privacy Act of 1974 (Privacy Act), 5 U.S.C.A. § 552a (West 2010), or the Freedom of Information Act (FOIA), 5 U.S.C. § 552 (2006 & Supp. III 2009), may otherwise be protected from disclosure by virtue of the privacy considerations due to victims under the CVRA. (*See* Article V.J.).

D. Mandatory Training

All Department personnel whose primary job responsibilities affect crime victims and witnesses shall have access to the AG Guidelines and complete a basic training session about the AG Guidelines, and statutory victims' services and rights, within a reasonable time after implementation of the AG Guidelines 2011 edition. Thereafter, all such employees shall receive the same access and training within a reasonable amount of time after assuming primary job responsibilities that impact crime victims and witnesses. Components should provide additional training on victim-related topics as necessary.

COMMENTARY

Components are encouraged to develop training in addition to the mandatory training required by this guideline. Such training can be more frequent, as with an annual or biannual basic training requirement, or can be tailored to specific job responsibilities or frequency of victim contact.

At the discretion of the component, Department personnel whose primary responsibilities are for civil cases and litigation may be exempted from this training requirement. If exempting personnel from the training, components should be mindful that some civil cases will have the potential to directly or indirectly affect crime victims, and personnel assigned to such cases should have at least a rudimentary understanding of the Department's obligations to victims.

E. Mandatory Reporting of AG Guidelines Compliance

The Director of the Office for Victims of Crime (OVC) has the statutory responsibility for monitoring Department compliance with the AG Guidelines. (42 U.S.C. § 10603(c)(3)(A) (2006 & Supp. III 2009)). Components shall report to the Attorney General, through the OVC Director, about their compliance by means of an Annual Compliance Report containing the relevant data (including the numbers of crime victims offered services) requested by the OVC Director. Unless directed otherwise by OVC, a component's Annual Compliance Report shall be submitted to OVC no later than April 20 of the fiscal year following the fiscal year that is the subject of the report.

F. AG Guidelines Compliance Measures

Each component shall devise and implement performance measures that will ensure component compliance with the AG Guidelines and the statutes upon which they are based. Implementation of compliance measures should be included in the component's Annual Compliance Report.

G. Performance Appraisal

The annual work plans and performance appraisals of each appropriate federal law enforcement officer, supervisor, investigator, prosecutor, corrections officer, and parole official (and appropriate staff of those agencies) shall encompass, as a required activity, implementation and evaluation of adherence or nonadherence with the victims' rights and victims' and witnesses' services provisions set forth in the AG Guidelines. All investigative, prosecutorial, correctional, and post-correctional components with responsibilities for providing rights and services to victims should include the discharge of such responsibilities among those components' criteria for reviews and evaluations. Verification of the institution of this recommendation must be included in the Annual Compliance Report.

[page intentionally left blank]

ARTICLE III

WHO IS A VICTIM

A. Introduction

Determining who qualifies as a victim may be one of the most difficult aspects of providing victim assistance. Federal statutes typically contain victim definitions applicable only to a particular statute's provisions. Two statutes describe the majority of the Department's responsibilities to crime victims. The first, the VRRA, mandates services to those directly harmed by a crime, while the CVRA establishes court-enforceable rights for those who are directly and proximately harmed by a charged offense. There are also separate victim definitions and unique requirements for particular types of victimization.

B. Victim Services Definition (VRRA Definition)

1. Basic Definition: For purposes of providing the services described in Article IV of these AG Guidelines, a victim is "a person that has suffered direct physical, emotional, or pecuniary harm as a result of the commission of a crime. . . ." (42 U.S.C. § 10607(e)(2)(A)).

2. Institutional Victims: If a victim is an institutional entity, services should be provided to an authorized representative of the entity. (42 U.S.C. § 10607(e)(2)).

3. Representative Victims: If a victim is under 18 years of age, incompetent, incapacitated, or deceased, services should be provided to one of the following (in order of preference): a spouse, legal guardian, parent, child, sibling, another family member, or another person designated by the court. (42 U.S.C. § 10607(e)(2)(B)). An incapacitated victim is any victim who is unable to interact with Department personnel for the purpose of receiving services as a result of a cognitive impairment or other physical limitation, or because of physical restraint or disappearance. More than one representative victim can be identified and provided with services depending upon the circumstances. It is Department policy that under no circumstances shall a person culpable for the crime be treated as a representative victim.

4. Timing: Department responsibilities to crime victims begin as soon as possible after the detection of a crime at which they may be undertaken without interfering in the investigation. (42 U.S.C. § 10607(b)). Generally, this point in time is defined by the opening of a criminal investigation.

   In some situations, an investigation may be initiated at a point in time when it is still unclear whether a crime was committed. In those situations, personnel should follow the guidance of Article II.A.

The end point for Department services obligations may be difficult to determine, and personnel should use their discretion and sound judgment to assess whether an investigation or prosecution is finally concluded. At that point, Department personnel may continue to provide services to the extent permitted by law and with available resources.

C. Enforceable Victims' Rights Definition (CVRA Definition)

1. Basic Definition: For purposes of enforcing the rights discussed in Article V, a victim is "a person directly and proximately harmed as a result of the commission of a Federal offense or an offense in the District of Columbia" (18 U.S.C. § 3771(e)) if the offense is charged in federal district court or the Superior Court of the District of Columbia.

2. Institutional Victims: A victim may be a corporation, company, association, firm, partnership, society, or joint stock company. (*See* 1 U.S.C. § 1 (2006)).

3. Representative Victims: If a victim is under 18 years of age, incompetent, incapacitated, or deceased, a family member or legal guardian of the victim, a representative of the victim's estate or any other person so appointed by the court may exercise the victim's rights, but, in no event, shall the defendant serve as a guardian or representative for this purpose. (18 U.S.C. § 3771(e)). An incapacitated victim is any victim who is unable to interact with Department personnel as a result of a cognitive impairment or other physical limitation, or because of physical restraint or disappearance.

4. Timing: CVRA rights attach when criminal proceedings are initiated by complaint, information, or indictment. If the defendant is convicted, CVRA rights continue until criminal proceedings have ended. For example, CVRA rights continue through any period of incarceration and any term of supervised release, probation, community correction, alternatives to incarceration, or parole. Absent a conviction, a victim's CVRA rights cease when charges pertaining to that victim are dismissed either voluntarily or on the merits, or if the government declines to bring formal charges after filing a complaint.

5. Scope of the Offense: Because the particular charges filed in a case will define the group of individuals with CVRA rights, prosecutors should carefully consider the scope of the charged offense when crafting the charging document. Charging decisions are within the discretion of the prosecution, and an individual can qualify as a CVRA victim regardless of whether he or she is named in the indictment. In cases with CVRA victims, prosecutors should give consideration to CVRA compliance from the outset of the prosecution through its conclusion.

D. Harm

1. Direct and Proximate Harm

   Determining whether a person meets the harm element of the legal definition of victim under the VRRA or CVRA requires a fact-specific analysis of both the nature of the harm allegedly suffered by the person and the crime that is alleged to have caused the harm. To qualify as a victim, both statutes require the alleged harm must be a direct consequence of the crime; that is, the harm must generally be a "but for" consequence of the conduct that constitutes the crime, specifically the crime under investigation, that has been charged, or for which there has been a conviction, depending on the stage of the criminal justice process. Intervening or contributing actions of the person suffering harm, or of a third party, may preclude a determination that the crimes being investigated or the offense charged directly caused the harm.

The CVRA requires an additional showing that the alleged harm must have been proximately caused by the offense. This showing ordinarily requires that the alleged harm must have been a reasonably foreseeable result of the charged offense. If both conditions are met, the person at issue meets the CVRA harm element.

COMMENTARY

Children who are depicted in child pornography that has been advertised, transported, distributed, received, accessed, or possessed are presumed to have been directly and proximately harmed as a result of those crimes for purposes of determining whether they are a victim under the VRRA or CVRA.

There may be instances in which case law developed in other legal contexts should be considered when determining issues of direct and proximate harm. For example, jurisprudence concerning direct versus indirect purchasers, as well as subject matter jurisdiction, under the antitrust laws is relevant to the issue of when a person injured by an antitrust violation has suffered the requisite harm under the VRRA and the CVRA.

There may also be instances in cases involving tax administration or other financial crimes in which a person, not charged with an offense, suffers harm due in part to their own willful participation in a scheme or transaction. Knowing and willful participation in such a scheme or transaction generally negates a determination of direct harm from the financial crimes being investigated or offense charged.

2. Types of Harm

    The harm can be physical, emotional, or pecuniary. In the absence of physical or pecuniary harm, emotional harm may be presumed in violent crime cases where the individual was actually present during a crime of violence, or, if not present, received information about a violent act attempted against him or her. In all other cases, emotional harm should not be presumed in the absence of physical or pecuniary harm, but rather the existence of cognizable emotional harm should be determined on a factual, case-by-case basis.

COMMENTARY

The impact of witnessing traumatic events involving loss of life and violent injury – along with the belief that one's own life will be taken – cannot be understated. Emotional injury may result in a range of physiological and psychological reactions, from temporary impairment in the ability of victims to cope and function to acute stress reactions and post-traumatic stress disorder. Visual imagery related to the event and the emotional and physical reactions associated with reliving the experience may remain with victims for many

COMMENTARY (CONTINUED)

years. The role of victim assistance personnel in investigative agencies is particularly critical to ensuring victims who suffer emotional injury receive timely intervention, information, and referrals. Later, criminal justice proceedings may reopen emotional wounds, and timely and appropriate assistance from prosecution-based victim assistance personnel can help meet victims' needs at this critical stage. In situations involving victims under 18 years of age who may have suffered emotional injury, victim assistance personnel will need to involve a parent or guardian in the provision of appropriate services.

In cases involving tax administration or other financial crimes, such as a tax shelter investigation, harm should not be presumed merely because participants paid a fee to the promoter for participation or for some fraudulent benefit promised but not received. In such cases, a determination that a participant suffered harm should be based on all of the facts and circumstances. For additional guidance, contact the Tax Division.

3. Harm in Identity Theft Cases

Determining harm in identity theft cases can be particularly difficult. Where Department personnel discover that a suspect possesses an individual's personally identifying information (PII), personnel should determine, based on the facts known at the time and any reasonable additional investigation, whether the PII was used in a way that could cause harm to the individual. If no evidence indicates that the information was misused, there is likely no direct harm to support victim status. If resources permit, Department personnel may notify such individuals that their information was compromised to allow the individuals to take appropriate measures to protect their credit.

If it appears that an individual's PII was used by the suspect or others in committing a crime, Department personnel should determine whether the individual suffered direct harm as a result of the misuse. Direct harm in these situations is usually pecuniary and may include out-of-pocket losses as well as time reasonably spent in an attempt to remediate actual or intended harm. In extraordinary cases, there may be solely or primarily emotional harm, such as harm to reputation from a false arrest that is a direct result of the misuse, with negligible or no pecuniary harm. Department personnel should consider the nature and extent of emotional harm when evaluating whether an individual should be classified as a victim for purposes of victims' rights and services.

In a large data breach case, the suspect or suspects may obtain PII for thousands or even millions of individuals. If there is no indication from the facts known at the time and any reasonable additional investigation that the information has been misused, then the direct harm may only be to the entity that legitimately held the PII. That entity may have suffered pecuniary harm as a result of having to respond to the data breach, and, if so, would fall within the definition of victim for the purposes of obtaining victim services and exercising victim rights (unless it is a governmental entity and therefore outside the definition of victim (*see* Article III.G.)). In such situations, state laws or civil court orders may obligate the entity to inform the individuals whose information was compromised so that they may take any action they deem appropriate to protect their credit.

Department personnel should encourage entities to notify individuals, with or without legal mandates, or, if resources permit, take steps themselves to notify such individuals that their information was compromised to allow the individuals to take appropriate measures to protect their credit.

E. Other Persons Affected by a Crime

In some cases there may be persons who do not fall under any statutory definition of crime victim but who nevertheless are affected by the criminal justice process concerning a defendant. Department personnel may provide such persons with appropriate assistance within available resources. To the extent permitted by law, and consistent with the interests of the United States in a particular case, persons who do not fit the CVRA definition of crime victim may be accommodated in their desire to participate in court proceedings or obtain information about the prosecution.

COMMENTARY

Examples of such persons include, but are not limited to, the following:

In a prosecution of a felon in possession of a firearm, a person known to Department personnel to have a credible reason to fear the defendant's gun possession, such as a known domestic violence victim who had been threatened with harm by the defendant, may be provided with assistance in connection with the possessory crime prosecution.

In a prosecution for immigration fraud based on misrepresentations about participation in the torture of others, witnesses testifying that the defendant had perpetrated torture upon them may be provided with assistance in connection with the immigration fraud prosecution.

F. Culpability

A person who is culpable for or accused of the crime being investigated or prosecuted should not be considered a victim for purposes of the rights and services described in the AG Guidelines. The determination of whether a person is culpable should be based on the facts and circumstances known at the time of investigation, prosecution, or post-conviction, and should be reevaluated as additional facts and circumstances become known. A person who may be culpable for violations or crimes other than the crime being investigated or prosecuted may be considered a victim under this policy in some circumstances.

Inmates who are victims of crime during their incarceration for other offenses may be considered victims. An inmate's detention, however, may prevent the inmate from exercising the rights and receiving the services normally afforded to victims. For example, Department personnel are not required by the AG Guidelines to transport inmates to court to attend hearings relating to crimes against those inmates.

COMMENTARY

Victims of involuntary servitude or trafficking may be considered victims for purposes of the prosecution of those crimes despite any legal culpability that the victims may have for ancillary offenses, such as immigration or prostitution crimes. A witness who is threatened or injured as the result of an attempt by another person to prevent the witness from cooperating with law enforcement or testifying before a grand jury or in court should be treated as a victim of the intimidation crime even though the witness may have some culpability in the matter about which he or she was testifying.

In contrast, individuals who are knowing and willful participants in an illegal tax shelter or other financial fraud are generally not considered victims of the crimes charged against the shelter or fraud promoters, even when the individuals are not criminally culpable for the charged crimes or any of the crimes under investigation. See Article III.D's commentary discussion regarding willful participation in a fraudulent scheme.

G. Government Entities

Neither the federal government nor any state, local, tribal, or foreign government or agency thereof fall under the definition of crime victim for either mandatory services or court-enforceable rights; however, they may qualify for restitution under federal restitution statutes. *See* 18 U.S.C. § 3664(i) (2006 & Supp. II 2008). Department personnel in their discretion may provide assistance to these entities pursuant to the policy contained in section E of this Article. Nothing herein is intended to prevent a government employee from asserting rights or receiving services as a victim of crime, even if such crime against the employee arose out of that employee's duties.

H. Victims in a Foreign Country and Foreign Nationality Victims

The victims' services and rights laws apply to foreign nationals meeting the definitions of victim under the VRRA and CVRA, regardless of whether they reside in the United States. Each country has its own procedures and requirements for contacting persons located in its territory. Due to sovereignty concerns, many countries limit or prohibit foreign government officials from directly contacting persons within that country's borders. Therefore, contact with victims and witnesses residing in other countries, for any purpose, needs to be coordinated with the appropriate officials of the host government through either the Department's Office of International Affairs (OIA) or the United States investigative attaché in the country where the victim resides. If victims in other countries do not have the ability to speak or read English, Department personnel should arrange for written communications to be translated. Because the coordination process can take several weeks, Department personnel should allow for extra time to notify victims in foreign countries. In cases with large numbers of victims, where Department personnel are using alternate means of notification, such as publication notice through media outlets or on a public Web site, coordination with an investigative attaché or OIA might not be necessary unless using a foreign media outlet or entity.

There are various types of immigration relief available to victims or witnesses who assist in the investigation or prosecution of certain criminal activity. Department personnel shall not offer victims or witnesses legal advice about immigration relief issues. If a victim or witness is pursuing legal status, Department personnel should provide, when warranted by the circumstances, the supporting documentation that must come from law enforcement.

Department personnel should inform the prosecutor immediately about any immigration relief issues in the case. Department personnel should be aware that immigration relief may constitute a benefit to the victim or witness, and this benefit may be subject to disclosure if the victim or witness testifies at trial.

COMMENTARY

Department personnel seeking to fulfill victim notification responsibilities should consult the OIA attorney responsible for handling matters in the country where the victim resides to obtain guidance and approval for appropriate victim notification procedures. In addition, Federal Bureau of Investigation (FBI), Drug Enforcement Administration (DEA), or other investigative agency attaché stationed abroad, and assigned to United States Embassies in countries with which the United States has diplomatic relations, may have information regarding appropriate notification procedures for victims residing in those countries.

Immigration relief for victims or witnesses may include an S–5 visa, U visa, or T visa. *See* S–5 visa (8 U.S.C. § 1101(a)(15)(S) (2006 & Supp. III 2009)); U visa (8 U.S.C. §§ 1101(a)(15)(U), 1184(p), 1255(l)); and, T visa (8 U.S.C. § 1101(a)(15)(T)).

I. Foreign Proceedings

Some crimes perpetrated in foreign countries or by persons located in foreign countries are also subject to United States jurisdiction. When a crime being investigated or prosecuted in the United States is also the subject of a foreign investigation or prosecution, victims in the United States investigation/prosecution may need assistance in obtaining information about and participating in the foreign prosecution. Department personnel may assist victims in the United States investigation/prosecution with information about foreign prosecutions and facilitate participation therein when appropriate and feasible with available resources.

J. Victims of Juvenile Offenders

Generally, victims of juvenile offenders are victims for purposes of the VRRA, CVRA, and the AG Guidelines, but the Federal Juvenile Delinquency Act (FJDA) (18 U.S.C. §§ 5031-5042 (2006)) restricts the type of information that may be disclosed to victims about investigations and proceedings regarding juvenile offenders unless the juvenile waives the restrictions or has been transferred for criminal prosecution as an adult. This law limits the statutory CVRA rights normally provided to victims.

1. Victim Services

   During the investigative stage, a crime victim should receive the services to which the victim would normally be entitled, but only a general statement about the progress of an investigation into the role of a juvenile suspect may be disclosed. Investigators and other Department personnel are cautioned that the name and other identifying data about a suspect who is known or believed to have been younger than 18 when the crime occurred should not be disclosed.

2. Victim Rights Available in Juvenile Cases

In federal juvenile delinquency proceedings, the FJDA nondisclosure provisions circumscribe victims' ability to exercise many CVRA rights. (*Compare* 18 U.S.C. § 3771(a)(2)-(4) *with* 18 U.S.C. § 5038(a)). Nonetheless, victims can, as in other criminal cases, be offered reasonable protection when needed (18 U.S.C. § 3771(a)(1)); confer with the attorney for the government (18 U.S.C. § 3771(a)(5)); and make known their injuries and views on appropriate disposition including whether the prosecutor should move to detain, dismiss, defer prosecution, move to transfer to adult status or accept a plea, and how severe a sentence is warranted. Prosecutors should inform victims that presentence reports and victim impact statements are not mandated at dispositional hearings but that a victim may prepare such a statement for the prosecutor to offer to the court. The prosecutor may also request that the court order the probation office to prepare a victim impact statement. Victims may be entitled to full and timely restitution (18 U.S.C. § 3771(a)(6); 18 U.S.C. § 5037(a)), and have the right to be treated with fairness and respect for their dignity and privacy (18 U.S.C. § 3771(a)(8)). Prosecutors shall advise victims that they can seek the advice of a private attorney. (18 U.S.C. § 3771(c)(2)). Prosecutors are not permitted to convey to the victim any prosecutorial information about the progress of a juvenile proceeding unless the court makes a delinquency finding. After a finding of delinquency, federal law explicitly permits disclosure, on request, of information about the final disposition to the victim or, if the victim is deceased, to the victim's immediate family. (18 U.S.C. § 5038(a)(6)). Upon request, a victim should be apprised of the final disposition of the case and the sentence imposed on the offender, but not the date when the juvenile offender in his or her case will be released from custody, unless the victim has requested such notification at that time.

K. Large Numbers of Victims

Cases with a large number of victims present unique challenges in affording victims' rights and services. While individual contact with victims is preferred, such contact may not be feasible as the number of victims grows into the hundreds and thousands. Department personnel should use new technology and be creative, with the goal of providing rights and services to the greatest extent possible given the circumstances and resources available. (*See* specific discussions in Article IV.E. (victim identification), V.D.2. (right to notice), V.E.4. (right not to be excluded from court), V.F. (right to be reasonably heard), and V.G.3. (right to confer)).

L. Particularly Vulnerable Victims

1. Child Victims

    a. Department Obligations

        (1) Department personnel should be aware of any obligations under applicable state, tribal, and federal law to report suspected child abuse.

(2) Department personnel should be aware that there are many statutory protections for child victims and witnesses. More extensive guidance about these protections and other promising practices are contained in other Departmental resources. Department personnel working on cases involving child victims and witnesses should review and become familiar with the protections contained in 18 U.S.C. § 3509 (2006 & Supp. III 2009) and other Department resources dealing with child victims and witnesses.

(3) Department personnel should be aware of the trauma that child victims and witnesses may experience when they are asked to relive the crime during the investigation and prosecution of a criminal case, particularly when testifying in court. A primary goal of Department personnel, therefore, shall be to reduce the potential trauma to child victims and witnesses that may result from their contact with the criminal justice system. To that end, Department personnel are required to provide age-appropriate support services to these victims, and referrals for community-based services to parents and guardians as indicated. (*See* Article IV.H.).

b. Definitions

(1) Child: For purposes of the AG Guidelines, a child is a person under the age of 18 years. For guidance on notifying child victims after they reach the age of majority, *see* Article IV.I.5.

(2) Child Abuse: For the purposes of this section, "child abuse" means the physical or mental injury, sexual abuse or sexual exploitation, or negligent treatment of a child. "Sexual abuse" includes rape, molestation, or incest with children. "Sexual exploitation" includes the production, distribution, receipt, possession, or access of child pornography, as well as the commercial sexual exploitation of children (prostitution), and the employment, use, persuasion, inducement, enticement, or coercion of a child to engage in, or assist another person to engage in, sexual abuse or sexual exploitation of children. The term "negligent treatment" means the failure to provide, for reasons other than poverty, adequate food, clothing, shelter, or medical care so as to seriously endanger the physical health of the child. "The term 'child abuse' does not include discipline administered by a parent or legal guardian to his or her child provided it is reasonable in manner and moderate in degree and otherwise does not constitute cruelty." (42 U.S.C. § 13031(c)(8) (2006)).

c. Child Abuse Reporting Requirements

(1) Report Suspected Child Abuse

Department personnel should promptly report suspected child abuse to a person designated to receive such reports in each office. This requirement is in addition to, not in place of, mandatory reporting requirements under state, tribal, and federal law with which Department personnel shall also comply.

(2) State Mandatory Reporting Laws

All Department personnel should refer to their state child abuse reporting laws to determine the scope of the obligation in cases of suspected child abuse. State laws vary substantially. Some states require mandatory reporting of child abuse or neglect by all persons within their boundaries; others require such reporting only from individuals engaged in expressly listed occupations. A report should be made even if the information inadvertently comes to the employee's attention, but not if the suspected child abuse has already been reported and is the subject of an existing report or investigation. Reports of child abuse required by state or local law shall be made to the agency or entity identified in accordance with that law.

(3) Federal Reporting Requirement

(a) Mandated Reporters

The federal child abuse reporting law requires certain professionals (including law enforcement personnel, probation officers, criminal prosecutors, juvenile rehabilitation or detention facility employees, and social workers) working on federal land or in a federally operated (or contracted) facility ~~in which children are cared for or reside,~~ to report suspected child abuse to an investigative agency designated by the Attorney General to receive and investigate such reports. (42 U.S.C. § 13031(a)).

(b) Sanctions for Failure To Report

A covered professional who, while working on federal land or in a federally operated (or contracted) facility ~~in which children are cared for or reside~~, learns of facts that give reason to suspect that a child has suffered an incident of child abuse and fails to timely report shall be fined or imprisoned not more than one year or both. (18 U.S.C. § 2258 (2006)).

(c) Agencies Designated by the Attorney General To Receive Reports

Reports of child abuse ~~on federal lands or in federally operated (or contracted) facilities~~ pursuant to 42 U.S.C. § 13031 shall be made to the local law enforcement agency or local child protective services agency that has jurisdiction to investigate reports of child abuse or to protect child abuse victims in the area or facility in question. When no such agency has entered into a formal written agreement with the Attorney General to investigate such reports, the FBI shall receive and investigate such reports. (28 C.F.R. § 81.3 (2010)).

(4) Reporting Child Abuse in Indian Country

Reporting child abuse in Indian Country is governed by 18 U.S.C. § 1169 (2006) and 25 U.S.C. § 3203 (2006). Covered professionals shall report suspected cases of child abuse to the federal, state, or tribal agency with primary responsibility for child protection or investigation of child abuse within the portion of Indian Country involved. If the report involves a potential crime and either involves an Indian child or an Indian suspect, the local law enforcement agency is required to make an immediate report to the FBI. (25 U.S.C. § 3203(b)(2)).

(5) Immediate Reports

The report of suspected child abuse should be made by a method best suited to giving immediate notice. According to 42 U.S.C. § 13031(e), use of a standardized form is encouraged, but shall not take the place of the immediate making of reports by other means when circumstances dictate. Reports may be made anonymously. Reports are presumed to have been made in good faith and reporters are immune from civil and criminal liability arising from the report unless they act in bad faith. (42 U.S.C. § 13031(f)). Reporters should document their report in the same manner that they document other important work-related actions.

(6) Child Abuse Discovered From a Confidential Source or Investigation

When Department personnel suspect that a child is being abused based on information gathered during a confidential investigation or from a confidential source, they should make every effort to report the abuse to the appropriate authorities in order to protect the safety of the child. If it is not possible to report the suspected child abuse without significantly compromising the investigation or other confidential source such as classified information, or endangering public safety, Department personnel shall obtain guidance from the designated component responsible official. (*See* Article IV.B. for a listing of component responsible officials). The component responsible official shall not delegate this responsibility. Component responsible officials are encouraged to consult personnel with expertise in the subject matter of child abuse and should be aware of the penalties, some of them criminal, that could result from a decision not to report.

d. Privacy Protections for Child Victims and Witnesses

Department personnel should scrupulously protect children's privacy in accordance with 18 U.S.C. § 3509(d), the AG Guidelines, and other Departmental policies. A child's name or other identifying information (other than initials or an alias) should not be reflected in court documents or other public records unless otherwise required by law.

(1) Motion To Render Nonphysical Identifying Information Inadmissible

Federal prosecutors may move in any prosecution under Chapter 110 or section 1466A of title 18 for an order that the name, address, Social Security number, and other nonphysical identifying information (other than the age or approximate age) of any minor who is depicted in any child pornography shall not be admissible and may be redacted from otherwise admissible evidence. (18 U.S.C. § 2252A(e)) (2006 & Supp. III 2009).

(2) Sanctions for Violating the Disclosure Rules

A knowing or intentional violation of the privacy protection accorded children in 18 U.S.C. § 3509(d) is a criminal contempt punishable by not more than one year's imprisonment, or fine, or both. (18 U.S.C. § 403 (2006)).

e. Child Protections During Criminal Investigations

(1) Multidisciplinary Child Abuse Teams

A multidisciplinary child abuse team is a professional unit composed of representatives from health, social service, law enforcement, and legal service agencies to coordinate the assistance needed to handle cases of child abuse. (18 U.S.C. § 3509(a)(7)). The goals of the multidisciplinary team are (1) to minimize the number of interviews to which the child is subjected to reduce the risk of suggestibility in the interviewing process, (2) to provide needed services to the child, and (3) to monitor the child's safety and well-being.

A multidisciplinary child abuse team shall be used when feasible. (18 U.S.C. § 3509(g)(1)). Department personnel should use existing multidisciplinary teams in their local communities. Law enforcement personnel are encouraged to bring other professionals onto the teams. Local laws and guidelines concerning the teams may vary, and federal personnel should become familiar with the local provisions. If no multidisciplinary team is in place in a particular community, Department personnel should coordinate with the local Child Protective Services and other agencies and experts to assemble the expertise necessary to ensure the most effective response to the crime and victim.

(2) Investigation/Forensic Interviewing of Child Victims and Witnesses

The first investigator responding to a report of child abuse or sexual abuse shall refer the child victim for a medical examination. Whenever possible, interviews of child victims and witnesses should be conducted by personnel properly trained in the techniques designed to best elicit truthful information from a child while minimizing additional trauma to the child.

COMMENTARY

Evidence from medical examinations and forensic interviews of children may provide the only corroboration for a successful prosecution of the case, particularly in cases of child abuse. Medical examinations provide documentation of the event and injuries, and forensic interviews gather factual information from a child to determine if the child was the victim of a crime or witnessed a crime against another person. The forensic interview should be appropriate for the child's age and developmental level, but it should not be confused with a therapeutic interview that is conducted for the purpose of designing treatment for and providing treatment to a child.

(3) Address Child Well-Being

Investigators should consider and make inquiry into whether children will be on the scene of an arrest, search warrant, or other enforcement action, and take appropriate actions to address the safety and well-being of children to include involving victim specialists or local child protection agencies as indicated by the circumstances and condition of the children prior to or at the time of the law enforcement action.

COMMENTARY

When assessing a child's well-being, Department personnel should consider whether the child lives in or is exposed to an environment where drugs, including pharmaceuticals, are used, possessed, trafficked, diverted, or manufactured illegally. In such environments, children may experience or be at risk of experiencing physical, sexual, or emotional abuse; medical, educational, emotional, or physical harm; or neglect, including harm resulting or possibly resulting from the inhalation, ingestion, or absorption of illegal drugs. Further, such environments may foster other crimes involving children. For example, children may participate in illegal or sexual activity in exchange for drugs or money likely to be used to purchase drugs.

f. Child Protections During Judicial Proceedings

(1) Child Witnesses

Section 3509 of title 18 provides mechanisms for the protection of child witnesses during judicial proceedings, including closing the courtroom during a child's testimony or allowing the child to testify via alternative means, allowing the use of adult attendants or testimonial aids, and expediting proceedings. Those prosecuting cases involving children should review and are urged to become familiar with the accommodations and protections under applicable law and use them as necessary to protect the interests of child witnesses.

A child is presumed to be competent. The court may permit an attorney, but not a party appearing *pro se,* to examine a child directly on competency, if the court is satisfied that the child will not suffer emotional trauma as a result of the examination. Federal prosecutors should consider making this request of the court because in many instances questioning by a familiar person may be less traumatic for the child. Prosecutors should, however, be aware that defense attorneys likewise may make such a request. (18 U.S.C. § 3509(c)(7)).

(2) Guardian ad Litem

To protect the best interests of the child, the court may appoint a guardian ad litem for a child who was a victim of, or a witness to, a crime involving abuse or exploitation. (18 U.S.C. § 3509(h)(1)). Although 18 U.S.C. § 3509(h) by its terms applies only to cases in which a child is a victim of or witness to abuse or exploitation, prosecutors should consider whether moving for the appointment of a guardian ad litem would be appropriate in any case in which a child is a victim of or witness to a crime.

(3) Victim Impact Statements

Department personnel should obtain and report to the probation officer accurate information concerning a child's victimization. Children may prepare victim impact statements. Child victim impact statements should be in an age-appropriate format that permits the child to express his or her views concerning the personal consequences of his or her victimization at a level and in a form of communication commensurate with his or her age and ability.

Department personnel should request information from the multidisciplinary child abuse team and other appropriate sources to determine the impact of the offense on the child victim and any other children who may have been affected, in order to provide the probation officer with the most useful and accurate information possible.

2. Victims of Domestic Violence, Sexual Assault, or Stalking

a. Statement of Purpose

Victims' rights laws and policies are of particular importance to victims of domestic violence, sexual assault, or stalking. These crimes often cause emotional trauma in addition to physical injury. It may be more difficult for victims to report these crimes because of the social stigma associated with the crimes and because the victims often have an on-going relationship with the offender. These victims often are in great danger of future violence after reporting a crime, during investigation and prosecution of cases, and after defendants are released from prison. Appropriate responses in these cases can save lives, prevent future violence, and promote victim recovery. Department personnel who work with victims of domestic violence, sexual assault, or stalking should recognize the particular vulnerability of these victims, use their best efforts to respect the privacy and dignity of these victims, and make victim safety a high priority.

b. Specific Guidelines

(1) Evidence of Past Sexual Behavior

Evidence about a victim's past sexual behavior or alleged sexual predisposition is generally inadmissible in court. Prosecutors should be aware of this evidentiary rule and use it when appropriate. (Fed. R. Evid. 412).

(2) Policy Strongly Discouraging Sexual Assault Victim Polygraphs

Department personnel are strongly discouraged from asking sexual assault victims to take polygraph examinations. The investigating agent may ask a sexual assault victim to take a polygraph examination only in extraordinary circumstances and only with the concurrence of a Special Agent in Charge or the Supervisory Assistant United States Attorney. All reasonable alternative investigative methods should be exhausted before requesting or administering a sexual assault victim polygraph examination.

(3) Referrals for Assistance in Developing a Safety Plan for Domestic Violence Victims

A safety plan is an individualized plan developed by domestic violence victims to reduce the threats of harm they and their family members face. Safety plans include strategies to reduce the risk of physical violence and harm (e.g., obtaining a protective order) and strategies to maintain basic human needs (e.g., housing and income) in spite of the disruptions caused by the victimization, which may include relocation, loss of employment, and physical injury. Victims may need assistance in identifying potential risks to safety and well-being, options for addressing those risks, and information about the types of services and support that may be required from the criminal justice system and community-based providers. Department personnel should consider providing referrals to community-based victim services programs to address those needs. Victim assistance personnel should also be familiar with any programs that exist in the jurisdiction that allow for confidentiality of the victim's address and the requirements for enrollment in those programs.

(4) Limited Testing of Defendants in Sexual Assault Cases

The responsible official shall advise a victim of a sexual assault that poses a "risk of transmission" of the Acquired Immune Deficiency Syndrome (AIDS) virus of the circumstances under which the victim may obtain an order that the defendant be tested for this condition and that the results be shared with the victim. (42 U.S.C. § 14011(b)(1) (2006)).

(5) Payment for Forensic Sexual Assault Examinations

The responsible official or the head of another department or agency that conducts an investigation into a sexual assault shall pay, either directly or by reimbursement to the victim, the cost of a physical examination of the victim and the costs of materials used to obtain evidence. (42 U.S.C. § 10607(c)(7)).

Department personnel should inform the sexual assault victim that he or she may choose to have the department or agency conducting the investigation pay the cost of the examination directly. In no case shall the victim be held responsible for payment for the examination or be required to seek reimbursement for the examination from his or her insurer. Moreover, in no case shall a victim of sexual assault be required to cooperate with law enforcement or prosecution in order to be provided with a forensic medical examination free of charge.

COMMENTARY

Many victims will be reluctant to obtain a forensic sexual assault examination if they know that their insurance company, primary policy holder, and possibly their employer or others will learn of the sexual assault; therefore victims should be informed that they may choose to have the department or agency conducting the sexual assault investigation directly pay the cost of the forensic medical examination.

At the time of an assault, the victim may not be prepared to make a decision to cooperate with the investigation and prosecution of a sexual assault case. Provision of the free forensic exam ensures the evidence is collected and will be available (i) should the victim decide to cooperate, (ii) if the government decides to prosecute without the victim's cooperation, or (iii) if the evidence is needed at a later date.

In cases of sexual assault in Indian Country, it is critically important that the investigative agency fulfill its responsibility to pay for forensic sexual assault examinations because other resources are unlikely to be available, and the absence of a forensic exam may hinder the ability of prosecutors to proceed with a criminal case.

(6) Availability of Payment for Testing and Counseling in Cases of Sexual Assault

The responsible official of the investigative agency shall inform victims of the Attorney General's obligation to pay the costs for up to two anonymous and confidential tests of the victim for sexually transmitted diseases during the 12 months following the assault, and to pay the cost of a counseling session by a medically trained professional regarding the accuracy of such tests and the risk of transmission of sexually transmitted disease to the victim as a result of the assault. (42 U.S.C. § 10607(c)(7)).

(7) Right To Make a Statement About Pretrial Release

The responsible official shall reasonably, and in a timely manner, inform a victim of an interstate domestic violence, violation of a protection order, or stalking offense that he or she has the right to make a statement regarding the danger posed by the defendant for the purpose of determining pretrial release of the defendant or the conditions of such release. (18 U.S.C. § 2263 (2006)).

(8) Mandatory Restitution

The Violence Against Women Act of 1994 (VAWA), Pub. L. No. 103-322, 108 Stat. 1796 (1994), requires courts to order full restitution in cases of sexual abuse (18 U.S.C. § 2248 (2006)) and interstate domestic violence, violation of a protection order, and stalking. (18 U.S.C. § 2264 (2006)).

(9) VAWA Self-Petitioning

VAWA's immigration provisions allow certain battered immigrants to file for immigration relief without their abusers' assistance or knowledge. This relief is available only for the spouses and children of U.S. citizens or aliens lawfully admitted for permanent residence. (8 U.S.C. § 1154 (2006 & Supp. III 2009)); (*see* Article III.H. for additional guidance on immigration relief).

3. Other Vulnerable Victims

a. Accommodation for Unique Vulnerabilities

Department personnel should be aware of the unique challenges that may be present when working with vulnerable victims and witnesses, such as the elderly and persons with physical and mental disabilities. These vulnerable victims and witnesses may have difficulty walking, hearing, or seeing, may be frail, on significant medications, or in chronic pain. Some may have an impaired level of cognitive function, dementia, depression, shame, ambivalence, or fear, which could cause them to be particularly vulnerable and anxious about the criminal justice system. For those vulnerable victims and witnesses who are disabled and homebound, prosecutors may consider the use of depositions, if feasible.

Department personnel should consider helping to make arrangements for transportation to and from court for those victims and witnesses who may not drive, have difficulty walking, or have other physical limitations that make it difficult to attend court proceedings. Arrangements should be made for wheelchairs and assistive listening devises, if needed. To the extent possible, Department personnel should make arrangements with the court in advance to accommodate physical limitations of victims and witnesses, if necessary.

b. Report Suspected Abuse

Whenever Department personnel suspect that an elderly or otherwise vulnerable adult victim or witness may be suffering from neglect, abuse, or exploitation (whether or not the individual is the subject of the matter being investigated or prosecuted), Department personnel should promptly contact the local Adult Protective Services agency or local law enforcement agency to report the concerns. The grounds for reporting such abuse may include physical evidence of abuse, sudden personality changes, disinterest in old habits, and signs of caregiver neglect. In addition, Department personnel should identify and provide referrals to appropriate local social service agencies best able to meet the needs of the victim. Department personnel should also be aware of possible nursing home abuse and report such to the Adult Protective Services or law enforcement agency, or to the state Attorney General's office.

[page intentionally left blank]

ARTICLE IV

MANDATORY SERVICES

A. Background

The VRRA mandates Department personnel to provide certain services to "crime victims" starting from the initiation of an investigation. The VRRA provisions are referred to as "services" to be distinguished from victims' "rights," which are contained in the CVRA and are covered in Article V. There is some overlap between rights and services, for example, "reasonable protection" is considered both a right and a service. Each statute, however, has its own definition of crime victim. (*See* Article III for the definitions under each statute). Accordingly, there may be some victims who qualify to receive services who will not be able to enforce crime victims' rights under the CVRA. This Article primarily addresses the VRRA victim services provisions.

B. Responsible Officials

The VRRA requires the Attorney General to designate persons in the Department of Justice who will be responsible for identifying the victims of a crime and performing the services described in that section at each stage of a criminal case. These persons are referred to as "responsible officials" in the statute and the AG Guidelines. (42 U.S.C. § 10607(a)). Responsible officials may delegate their responsibilities under the AG Guidelines to subordinates in appropriate circumstances, but responsible officials remain obligated to ensure that delegated responsibilities are discharged.

The Attorney General designates the following responsible officials:

1. Investigations

   a. Bureau of Alcohol, Tobacco, Firearms and Explosives (ATF); Drug Enforcement Administration (DEA), and the Federal Bureau of Investigation (FBI) – the Special Agent-in-Charge (SAC) of the division having primary responsibility for conducting the investigation.

   b. Office of the Inspector General (OIG) – the Inspector General; and

   c. United States Marshals Service (USMS) – the United States Marshal in whose district the case is being conducted.

2. Once Charges Are Filed

   The United States Attorney in whose district the prosecution is pending, unless a Department litigating division is solely litigating the case in which situation the responsible official is the section chief to whom the lead prosecutor reports. By mutual agreement, the United States Attorney and any Department litigating division can transfer responsible official status to the other entity. Agreements should be in writing and detail how victim obligations are to be fulfilled (see, e.g., Memorandum from the Acting Assistant Attorney General, Criminal Division, on implementing the Attorney General Guidelines for Victim and Witness Assistance to the Director, Executive Office for United States Attorneys (June 17, 1993)).

3. Corrections

For cases in which the Bureau of Prisons (BOP) has become involved – the Director or Warden of each BOP facility where the defendant/offender is incarcerated.

4. Parole

For proceedings relating to parole, parole revocation, release to supervision for all parole-eligible offenders, and supervised-release revocation for District of Columbia offenders – the Chairman of the United States Parole Commission.

The responsible official shall designate the personnel who will carry out victim services in each Department of Justice investigating field office, United States Attorney's Office, litigating division, corrections facility, and parole office. The responsible official shall instruct designated personnel to comply with the AG Guidelines and shall delegate to such personnel the authority to carry out the activities thereby required.

C. Timing of Services

Department responsibilities to crime victims begin as soon as possible after the detection of a crime at which they may be undertaken without interfering in the investigation. (42 U.S.C. § 10607(b)). Generally, this point in time is defined by the opening of a criminal investigation. (See Article III.B.4. for additional guidance on the time parameters for Department obligations.)

D. Coordination of Services

Department personnel should coordinate with each other in providing victims with the services required by federal law and the AG Guidelines.

The nature and extent of services provided may vary with the type of harm experienced by the victim and other surrounding circumstances. When victims require services provided by personnel from another Department component or other agency, Department personnel should appropriately coordinate with and introduce victims to other components' and agencies' victim assistance personnel. Introductions should include an explanation of each component's role. Department personnel should support each other as members of a team, coordinating services to the greatest possible extent, with a goal of providing consistent services to meet victims' needs.

E. Victim Identification

At the earliest opportunity after the detection of a crime at which it may be done without interfering with an investigation, the responsible official of the investigative agency shall identify the victims of the crime. (42 U.S.C. §10607(b)(1)). Basically, victim identification means identifying the names and contact information for victims. The responsibility for identifying victims continues with the investigative agency throughout the criminal justice process. Other Department components or other investigative agencies may also identify victims, but all identifications should be coordinated with the lead case agent.

For those components having access to the automated Victim Notification System (VNS), identified victims' names and contact information should be entered into VNS as soon as practicable, but no later than at criminal charging. In cases where the identified victim is less than 18 years old, Department personnel should enter the child's date of birth into VNS to facilitate notification when children (who may receive notification through parents or guardians) become adults and are entitled to direct notification. Non-VNS participating components should maintain victims' names and contact information in a format that can be easily converted to the VNS system should the investigation result in a prosecution.

Some specialized types of cases are not entered into VNS during the investigative stage. These include national security investigation/counterterrorism cases. In those cases, responsible officials from the investigative agency should record identified victims' names and contact information in another secure manner.

Identifying and locating victims can be one of the most difficult victim assistance tasks in a case with a large number of victims. Both new technology and traditional law enforcement methods can be utilized to identify victims. For example, officials may use notices on official Web sites or in print or broadcast media to ask victims to contact the agency. Access to a toll-free number can be arranged so that victims can both provide identification information and receive information about available assistance and services. Department employees may also work with hospitals, schools, employers, nonprofit organizations, faith-based organizations, and disaster-assistance centers (where appropriate) to reach out to victims and to secure identification and contact information. In large white-collar crime cases, names and addresses of victims may be obtainable from the defendants' records. For crimes involving aviation disasters, the FBI is the lead investigative agency and has specialized protocols for collecting passenger- and ground-casualty victim information.

F. Reasonable Protection

The investigative agency responsible official shall arrange for a victim to receive reasonable protection from a suspected offender and persons acting in concert with or at the behest of the suspected offender. (42 U.S.C. § 10607(c)(2)). Both the VRRA and the CVRA use the concept of "reasonable protection." (42 U.S.C. § 10607(c)(2); 18 U.S.C. § 3771(a)(1)). Accordingly, responsible officials shall take reasonable measures to address victims' legitimate security concerns. Determining the nature and scope of such measures requires an evaluation of the threat level and identification of reasonable options to address that threat within available resources. As with other rights and services, victims may choose to accept or decline any option or options offered by the Department. (*See* Article II.B.). Neither statute requires the Department to provide victims with, for example, bodyguards to ensure their physical security.

The responsibility of arranging for reasonable victim protection remains with the responsible official of the investigative agency throughout the criminal justice process. All Department personnel, however, should consider victims' security concerns at every point in the criminal justice system, and consult and coordinate with the responsible official of the investigative agency concerning victim safety. Any concerns about victim safety and reports of threats should immediately be reported to the lead case agent.

Department personnel should use their discretion and sound judgment when discussing possible threats and security measures with victims. Trained personnel should make victims aware of the resources that may be available to promote their safety. Responsible officials from the investigation, prosecution, and corrections components, as well as the United States Parole Commission, are encouraged to work together to meet the safety concerns of victims. United States Attorneys are encouraged and expected to work with designated responsible officials from investigative components to develop collaborative procedures to meet the safety concerns of victims in their districts.

G. General Information

After the investigative agency opens a case, a responsible official should provide victims with the following general information as needed:

1. Information About VNS: Victims should be informed that they will receive notification of case developments through VNS, and may decide at any time to opt out of receiving VNS notifications.

2. Logistical Information: Victims should be informed and assisted with respect to transportation, parking, childcare, translator services, and other investigation-related services. Once the prosecution agency files charges, the responsible official of the prosecution agency is responsible for informing and assisting victims with such information in connection with prosecution-related services. Even before the prosecution files charges, the responsible prosecution official should assist victims with logistical information in connection with pre-charging court proceedings such as grand jury appearances. The responsible official of the Parole Commission is responsible for informing and assisting victims with similar services in connection with parole hearings.

3. Department Employees Who Are Victims of Crime: The responsible officials of each agency should inform Department employees that they can access an Employee Assistance Program as well as generally available victim assistance programs. Responsible officials should assist employees in accessing appropriate victim services.

4. Information About the Criminal Justice System: During all stages of the process, a responsible official should provide statutory victims with general information about the criminal justice process, specifically including –

   a. Role: The role of the victim in the criminal justice process, including what the victim can expect from the system as well as what the system expects from the victim.

   b. Stages: The stages in the criminal justice process that are significant to a crime victim and the manner in which information about such stages can be obtained.

   (18 U.S.C. § 1512 note (1984) (Federal Guidelines for Treatment of Crime Victims and Witnesses in the Criminal Justice System); cf. Pub. L. No. 97-291, § 6(a)(1)(C), (D)).

5. Custodial Release Eligibility Information: A responsible official of the custodial agency shall provide the victim with general information regarding the corrections process, including information about work release, furlough, probation, and eligibility for each. (42 U.S.C. §10607(c)(8)).

H. Services Referrals

At the earliest opportunity after detection of a crime at which it may be done without interfering with an investigation, a responsible official shall provide identified victims with information about services available to them. (42 U.S.C. § 10607(b)(2)). The information shall include the name, title, business address, and telephone number of the responsible official to whom services requests should be addressed (42 U.S.C. § 10607(b)(3)), and the types of services available, including, as appropriate –

1. The place where the victim may receive emergency medical or social services. (42 U.S.C. § 10607(c)(1)(A)).

2. The availability of any restitution or other relief (including crime victim compensation programs) to which the victim may be entitled under this or any other applicable law and the manner in which such relief may be obtained. (42 U.S.C. § 10607(c)(1)(B)).

3. Public and private programs that are available to provide counseling, treatment, and other support to the victim. (42 U.S.C. § 10607(c)(1)(C)).

The responsibility for providing a victim with referrals for services during the investigation lies with the responsible official for the investigative agency. Once an investigation has transferred to the prosecutorial entity or charges are filed, responsible officials from the prosecutorial entity are responsible for ensuring referrals for services are made as appropriate. If a victim has already received referrals for services from the investigative agency, the prosecutorial entity and investigative agency shall employ their best efforts to coordinate any existing and new referrals to ensure consistency, avoid duplication of services, and meet the best interests of the victim and the case.

I. Notice of Case Events

1. During the Investigation

   During the investigation of a crime, a responsible official for the investigative agency shall provide the victim with the earliest possible notice concerning –

   a. The status of the investigation of the crime, to the extent that it is appropriate and will not interfere with the investigation. (42 U.S.C. § 10607(c)(3)(A)).

   b. The arrest of a suspected offender. (42 U.S.C. § 10607(c)(3)(B)).

2. During the Prosecution

   Responsible officials from the prosecutor's office shall provide notice of court-related case events to victims meeting the VRRA victim definition. (*See* definition in Article III.B.). The VRRA requires notice of the following case events:

   a. The filing of charges against a suspected offender. (42 U.S.C. § 10607(c)(3)(C)).

   b. The release or detention status of an offender or suspected offender. (42 U.S.C. § 10607(c)(3)(E)).

   c. The "scheduling of each court proceeding that the witness is either required to attend or . . . is entitled to attend." (42 U.S.C. § 10607(c)(3)(D)).

   d. The acceptance of a plea of guilty or nolo contendere or the rendering of a verdict after trial. (42 U.S.C. § 10607(c)(3)(F)).

   e. If the offender is convicted, the sentence including the date on which the offender will be eligible for parole, if any. (42 U.S.C. § 10607(c)(3)(G)).

COMMENTARY

Persons meeting the VRRA victim definition receiving investigative notices should continue to receive prosecution notification either through VNS or other means if VNS is not used. (*See generally* Article V.D.1. regarding VNS coverage). Notices should explain that only victims meeting the CVRA victim definition will be able to assert CVRA rights.

3. During the Corrections Process

   a. Custodial Release Notification

      After trial, a responsible official from the BOP shall provide a crime victim as defined under the VRRA (*see* Article III.A.) the earliest possible notice of –

      (1) The escape, work release, furlough, or any other form of release from custody of the offender. (42 U.S.C. § 10607(c)(5)(B)).

(2) The death of the offender, if the offender dies while in custody. (42 U.S.C. § 10607(c)(5)(C)).

b. Inmate Victims

When the victim is an inmate, the responsible official may take into consideration, in determining when notice is provided, the security of the offender inmate. If there is a serious security risk in informing an inmate victim of an offender's status, the corrections agency may time the notice to minimize that risk, even if the notification takes place after the event. This determination should be made on a case-by-case basis and should not be interpreted to prevent an inmate victim from providing written input in any parole proceeding. The notice requirement in this guideline applies even in cases in which a Department component is holding a defendant (such as a deportable alien) after time served.

c. Prisoner Reentry

In anticipation of an offender's release from custody, the BOP responsible official should take the following actions:

(1) Victim Impact Statement: If the offender is subject to supervised release in a district other than the district in which the offender was sentenced, the responsible official should transmit the victim impact statement portion of the presentence investigation report to the United States Probation Office in the supervising district.

(2) Notification Contents: The responsible official should provide a victim with notice of the offender's release date no later than 30 days prior to the offender's release. The notice should also include the city and state in which the offender will be released and, if the offender is subject to supervised release, the supervising United States Probation Office contact information. This notice should also advise the victim to contact the supervising United States Probation Office if the victim receives any threatening communications from the offender. (Note: This renewed notification should not be shared with the offender or his counsel, except as otherwise required by law.)

4. During the Parole Process

After conviction, the responsible official from the Parole Commission shall provide a crime victim as defined under the VRRA (*see* Article III.B.) with the earliest possible notice of the date on which an offender will be eligible for parole and the scheduling of a parole hearing, if any, for the offender. (42 U.S.C. § 10607(c)(3)(G), (c)(5)(A)).

When an offender violates the conditions of release and a revocation hearing is scheduled, the responsible official from the Parole Commission shall notify the victims of the crime for which parole was granted or supervised release was imposed of the date and time of the revocation proceeding. If the alleged violation is the commission of a new crime, whether or not the offender has been convicted of the crime, the Parole Commission responsible official should also notify the victims of the new crime.

The Parole Commission responsible official should notify victims in advance of an offender's release to supervision.

5. Victim's Age

Once a child victim reaches 18 years of age, the Department is obligated to provide that victim with notification in cases in which the crime occurred when the victim was a minor. It is also the victim's option to determine who else may receive notification on his or her behalf. Department personnel should take care when initiating the direct notifications, being mindful of the impact on the victim. Department personnel are encouraged to develop specialized procedures to deal with these sensitive situations. In general, Department personnel are encouraged to contact a parent or guardian before the victim's 18th birthday to determine whether the victim is aware of the crime and any special considerations that may be helpful in providing notification. The FBI has developed specialized victim notification procedures for cases involving child pornography. Any Department personnel making notifications in such cases are encouraged to coordinate with the FBI.

J. Separate Waiting Area

During court proceedings, the responsible official shall ensure that a victim is provided with a waiting area removed from and out of the sight and hearing of the defendant and defense witnesses. (42 U.S.C. § 10607(c)(4)).

During parole hearings, the responsible official should coordinate with the United States Marshals Service, BOP, or other entity responsible for the relevant facilities to ensure that a victim is provided with a waiting area that is removed from and out of the sight and hearing of the inmate and the inmate's witnesses. (*See* 42 U.S.C. § 10607(c)(4)).

K. Return of Property

A responsible official from the investigative agency shall ensure that any property of a victim that is being held for evidentiary purposes is maintained in good condition and returned to the victim as soon as it is no longer needed for evidentiary purposes. (42 U.S.C. § 10607(c)(6)). The responsible official from the investigative agency should also, where it does not interfere with the investigation, notify victims that the agency is holding property belonging to the victim. There may be circumstances, however, in which a victim's property will inevitably deteriorate or will be damaged through its utilization in the law enforcement process. Responsible officials may consider advising victims of such circumstances when they arise. Contraband should not be returned to victims.

L. Employer/Debt Notification

Upon request by a victim, the responsible official should assist in notifying –

1. The employer of the victim or witness if cooperation in the investigation/prosecution of the crime causes his or her absence from work.

2. The creditors of the victim or witness, when appropriate, if the crime or cooperation in the investigation/prosecution affects his or her ability to make timely payments.

Upon filing of charges by the prosecutor, this responsibility transfers to the responsible official of the prosecutor's office.

(*See* 18 U.S.C. § 1512 note (1984) (Federal Guidelines for Treatment of Crime Victims and Witnesses in the Criminal Justice System)).

[page intentionally left blank]

ARTICLE V

VICTIMS' RIGHTS UNDER THE CVRA

A. Background

The CVRA gives victims in criminal cases eight rights that are enforceable in federal courts. The CVRA "rights" should be distinguished from crime victim "services" contained in VRRA, which mandates Department personnel to provide certain services to crime victims starting from the initiation of an investigation. (*See* Article IV.). There is some overlap between the rights and services. For example, "reasonable protection" is considered both a right and a service. Each statute, however, has its own definition of "crime victim." (*See* Article III for the definitions under each statute). Accordingly, there may be some victims who qualify to receive services, but who will not have court enforceable rights under the CVRA. This Article primarily addresses the victims' rights provisions contained in the CVRA.

B. Responsibilities of Department Personnel

1. Best Efforts

   Department officers and employees engaged in the detection, investigation, or prosecution of crime shall make their best efforts to see that crime victims (as defined in Article III.C.) are notified of, and accorded, the rights contained in the CVRA (18 U.S.C. § 3771(c)(1)) as early in the criminal justice process as is feasible and appropriate.

2. Advice of Attorney

   The prosecutor shall advise the crime victim that the crime victim can seek the advice of an attorney with respect to the CVRA rights. (18 U.S.C. § 3771 (c)(2)). The prosecutor should provide this information as early in the criminal justice process as is feasible and appropriate.

3. Professional Responsibility Considerations

   Department attorneys should keep the rules of professional conduct in mind in all interactions with crime victims, including while according crime victims their rights under the CVRA. While the American Bar Association Model Rules of Professional Conduct are referenced below, Department attorneys should consider the specific rules applicable to their conduct, determined by their state(s) of licensure as well as where the case or investigation is proceeding.

   Responsible officials should make reasonable efforts to train and properly instruct the non-attorneys who interact with crime victims about attorneys' obligations under the rules of professional conduct and to ensure non-attorneys' conduct is compatible with those rules. (*See* Model Rules of Prof'l Conduct R. 5.3(b)). In addition, all Department attorneys should keep in mind that they can be held accountable, for professional responsibility purposes, for the conduct of non-attorneys with whom they work. (*See* Model Rulesof Prof'l Conduct R. 5.3(c)).

Specifically, Department attorneys should inform crime victims that they do not have an attorney-client relationship with any employee of the Department. Likewise, in dealing with crime victims, Department attorneys should keep in mind their duty of confidentiality to their client, the United States, and not disclose any confidential information of the United States unless the United States consents or the disclosure is impliedly authorized to carry out the representation, including disclosures impliedly authorized as required by the CVRA. (*See* Model Rules of Prof'l Conduct R. 1.6).

When dealing with unrepresented victims, Department attorneys should make their role clear, should not state or imply that they are disinterested, and should not give legal advice other than to advise individuals to seek legal counsel. (*See* Model Rules of Prof'l Conduct R. 4.3).

A crime victim may seek the legal advice of a non-Department attorney with respect to CVRA rights, and the CVRA provides that the prosecutor shall inform the crime victim that the crime victim may seek the advice of an attorney with respect to the rights contained in the CVRA. (18 U.S.C. § 3771(c)(2)). When a crime victim is represented on the criminal matter, a Department attorney should consider the professional responsibility issues involved in *ex parte* communication with a represented party. Generally, *ex parte* communication with a represented crime victim may be authorized by the CVRA statute to carry out the Department's responsibilities to crime victims as well as authorized by law to carry out investigative activities. (*See* Model Rules of Prof'l Conduct R. 4.2).

When Department personnel consider providing victim notification by means that are accessible by the general public, for example, through an unsecure Web site or at an open town hall meeting, personnel should only disclose information that comports with Department and professional responsibility rules limitations. (*See* Model Rules of Prof'l Conduct R. 3.6, 3.8(f)). For guidance in particular cases, Department attorneys should consult their Professional Responsibility Officer or the Department's Professional Responsibility Advisory Office.

4. Complaint Process and Sanctions

The Department established the Office of the Victims' Rights Ombudsman (VRO), within the Executive Office for United States Attorneys, to receive and investigate administrative complaints filed by crime victims against its employees, and has implemented procedures in compliance with the CVRA. (Procedures to Promote Compliance With Crime Victims' Rights Obligations, 28 C.F.R. § 45.10(b) (2010)). The complaint process is not designed for the correction of an individual victim's rights violation, but is instead used to request corrective or disciplinary action against Department employees who may have failed to provide crime victims with any of the CVRA rights. A crime victim may file an administrative complaint against employees of the Department. All of the following offices have identified Victims' Rights Points of Contact, who are responsible for reviewing and investigating victims' complaints, and reporting their results to the VRO for final determination: United States Attorneys' Offices, the Antitrust Division, ATF, BOP, Civil Division's Office of Consumer Litigation, Civil Rights Division, Criminal Division, DEA, Environment and Natural Resources Division, FBI, National Security Division, Tax Division, Parole Commission, and the USMS. The VRO may recommend disciplinary sanctions for Department employees who "wantonly or willfully" fail to provide those rights. (28 C.F.R. § 45.10(e)).

C. Right to Reasonable Protection

A crime victim has the right to be reasonably protected from the accused. (18 U.S.C. § 3771(a)(1)).

Both the CVRA and the VRRA use the concept of "reasonable protection." (42 U.S.C. § 10607(c)(2); 18 U.S.C. § 3771(a)(1)). Accordingly, responsible officials shall take reasonable measures to address victims' legitimate security concerns. Determining the nature and scope of such measures requires an evaluation of the threat level and identification of reasonable options to address that threat within available resources. As with other rights and services, victims may choose to accept or decline any option or options offered by the Department. (*See* Article II.B.). Neither statute requires the Department to provide victims with, for example, bodyguards to ensure their physical security.

The responsibility of arranging reasonable victim protection remains with the responsible official of the investigative agency throughout the criminal justice process. All Department personnel, however, should consider victims' security concerns at every point in the criminal justice system, and consult and coordinate with the responsible official of the investigative agency concerning victim safety. Any concerns about victim safety and reports of threats should immediately be reported to the lead case agent.

Department personnel should use their discretion and sound judgment when discussing possible threats and security measures with victims. Trained personnel should make victims aware of the resources that may be available to promote their safety.

Responsible officials from the investigation, prosecution, and corrections components, as well as the Parole Commission, are encouraged to work together to meet the safety concerns of victims. U.S. Attorneys are encouraged and expected to work with designated responsible officials from investigative agencies to develop collaborative procedures to meet the safety concerns of victims in their districts.

D. Right to Reasonable, Accurate, and Timely Notice

A crime victim has the right to reasonable, accurate, and timely notice of any public court proceeding, or any parole proceeding, involving the crime or of any release or escape of the accused. (18 U.S.C. § 3771(a)(2); *see also* Fed. R. Crim. P. 60(a)(1)).

1. Automated Victim Notification System (VNS)

   For components participating in VNS, victim contact information and notice to victims should be maintained and conducted using VNS. In some circumstances, however, either alternative or additional means of victim notification may be necessary or appropriate. For example, during terrorism investigations VNS is not used, and in some situations, like Indian Country, victims may not have access to postal or computer systems, thereby making VNS impractical.

   Responsible officials with access to VNS should enter all necessary information into VNS before transferring notification responsibilities to the next responsible official. In cases where the identified victim is a child, the child's date of birth should be entered into VNS. For specialized guidance on notifying child victims once they become adults, *see* Article IV.I.5. Responsible officials shall use their best efforts to provide all employees with responsibilities related to VNS with adequate training on the proper use of VNS. (*See* Article III.F. for information about notifying victims located in foreign countries).

   In the event of an emergency or other last-minute hearing or change in the time or date of a hearing, the responsible official should consider providing notice by telephone or expedited means.

2. Cases With Large Numbers of Victims

   a. Individual Notice

      According the right to notification in cases with a large number of victims can be challenging. When necessary, Department employees may choose to provide notification solely through electronic means such as via the VNS Web site, e-mail, and call center capabilities.

   b. Publication or Proxy Notice

      Where the number of victims is so large as to make individual notice to victims impractical, prosecutors should file a motion seeking the court's permission for alternative notification under 18 U.S.C. § 3771(d)(2). Such alternative notification may include publication of notices through media outlets or on public Web sites, or proxy notification to an individual or organization that can disseminate notice to other victims, such as community organizations, corporate entities, or counsel for a class of victims. Multiple forms of outreach may be appropriate in particular cases and creativity is encouraged, with the goal of achieving actual notice to the greatest number of victims possible given the resources available. In every case, Department employees should carefully evaluate the type of information relayed and the method of communication to minimize the risk that investigations are compromised and that victims' privacy interests are inadvertently invaded.

E. Right Not To Be Excluded From Court

A crime victim has the right not to be excluded from any public court proceeding, unless the court, after receiving clear and convincing evidence, determines that testimony by the victim would be materially altered if the victim heard other testimony at that proceeding. (18 U.S.C. § 3771(a)(3); *see also* Fed. R. Crim. P. 60(a)(2)). Before making this determination, "the court shall make every effort to permit the fullest attendance possible by the victim and shall consider reasonable alternatives to the exclusion of the victim from the criminal proceeding." (18 U.S.C. § 3771(b)(1); *see also* Fed. R. Crim. P. 60(a)(2)). The reason for any decision denying relief shall be clearly stated on the record. (18 U.S.C. § 3771(b)(1); *see also* Fed. R. Crim. P. 60(a)(2)).

1. Victims Who Are Also Witnesses

   The crime victim's right not to be excluded provides statutory authorization for an exception to the *Federal Rules of Evidence,* which mandate that, upon request, the judge exclude witnesses from court so that they cannot hear the testimony of other witnesses. (*See* Fed. R. Evid. 615(4)).

   If a victim is a witness, and there is a potential detrimental impact from the victim hearing other witnesses' testimony, prosecutors should explain any potential detrimental impact so that the victim can make an informed decision whether to exercise this right. If the prosecutor believes that the victim's testimony would be materially altered if the victim heard other testimony at the proceeding, the prosecutor should inform the victim of this potential divergence of interests and remind the victim that he or she can seek the advice of an attorney in connection with asserting the victim's rights.

   Where appropriate, prosecutors should also make courts aware of the provisions of 18 U.S.C. § 3510, which prohibits a court from ordering a victim excluded from a trial based only on the victim's exercise of his or her right to be heard during the sentencing hearing for both capital and non-capital cases.

2. Facilitating Attendance

   The Department is not required to pay a victim's expenses to attend court. Department personnel may, however, help victims to identify resources to assist them with the financial burden of court attendance. In addition, Department personnel are not required to transport inmate victims to court for hearings. The travel expenses of victims who are also witnesses, however, should be handled in accordance with Department policy for witness expenses.

3. Non-Public Proceedings

   Victims do not have rights to notice of, or to attend or participate in, closed official proceedings. (*See* 18 U.S.C. § 3771(a)(2)-(3)). The government attorney may neither move for nor consent to the closure of a judicial proceeding that is ordinarily open to the public without the express prior authorization of the Deputy Attorney General, based upon a request processed through the Policy and Statutory Enforcement Unit of the Criminal Division's Office of Enforcement Operations. (*See* Policy With Regard to Open Judicial Proceedings, 28 C.F.R. § 50.9 (2010); USAM 9-5.150). As an example of the type of ordinarily public proceeding falling in this category, closed proceedings will frequently be necessary when a guilty plea is entered by a cooperator whose safety or investigative usefulness might be compromised if information about the plea were made public. Deputy Attorney General approval to close a hearing is not required for traditionally non-public matters, such as grand jury and juvenile proceedings; to prevent psychological harm to a child witness (*see* 18 U.S.C. § 3509(d), (e); 28 C.F.R. § 50.9(e)(5)); and to protect national security information or classified documents. Victims do not have rights to notice of, or attendance or participation at, these closed hearings.

4. Cases With Large Numbers of Victims

In cases with a large number of victims, it may be impractical for each victim to attend personally all the proceedings he or she may wish to attend. In such circumstances, prosecutors should seek the court's permission under 18 U.S.C. § 3771(d)(2) for procedures to accord this right to the greatest extent possible given the resources available. Options include the use of closed circuit television, broadcast of proceedings over a conference call or Web site, or a lottery and schedule for attendance. If the court changes the trial venue, prosecutors should be aware of the provisions of 42 U.S.C. § 10608, which mandates the court to order closed-circuit televising of the proceedings to the original location to permit victims to watch the trial proceedings.

F. Right To Be Reasonably Heard

A crime victim has the right to be reasonably heard at any public proceeding in the district court involving release, plea, sentencing, or any parole proceeding. (18 U.S.C. § 3771(a)(4); *see also* Fed. R. Crim. P. 60(a)(3)).

If a victim (or a lawful representative appearing on behalf of the victim) is present at a covered proceeding and wishes to be heard, the government attorney or prosecutor should advise the court of this fact at an appropriate point in the proceeding. If the prosecutor is aware that a victim or victims will seek to be heard at an upcoming proceeding that involves release, plea, sentencing, or parole, the prosecutor should provide the court with advance notice in accordance with any local rules of procedure or practice.

If the government is seeking the death penalty, and files the proper notice, the responsible official should notify the victim and appropriate family members of their potential opportunity to address the court during the aggravation portion of the sentencing hearing and of the date, time, and place of the scheduled hearing. (*See* 18 U.S.C. § 3593(a) (2006)).

In cases with a large number of victims, it may be impractical for each victim to speak at each opportunity. In such circumstances, prosecutors should seek the court's permission under 18 U.S.C. § 3771(d)(2) for procedures to accord this right to the greatest extent possible given the resources available. Options may include allowing written submissions, limiting the length of oral presentation, or using a lottery or other method for selecting a limited number of oral statements.

When a defendant is convicted, Department personnel should inform victims that the United States probation officer is required to prepare a presentence investigation report that includes a section assessing the financial, social, psychological, and medical impact of the crime on any individual against whom the offense was committed, including restitution information. (Fed. R. Crim. P. 32(d)(2)(B), (D)). This section is called the Victim Impact Statement (VIS) and Department personnel should inform victims how to communicate directly with the probation officer concerning the VIS if victims choose to do so. Department personnel should also inform the probation officer about any information in the government's possession relevant to the topics addressed in the VIS, particularly concerning the appropriate amount of restitution, if any.

G. Reasonable Right To Confer With the Prosecutor

A crime victim has the reasonable right to confer with the attorney for the government in the case. (18 U.S.C. § 3771(a)(5)).

The victim's right to confer shall not be construed to impair prosecutorial discretion. (*See* 18 U.S.C. § 3771(d)(6)).

1. In General

    Federal prosecutors should be available to confer with victims about major case decisions, such as dismissals, release of the accused pending judicial proceedings (when such release is for non-investigative purposes), plea negotiations, and pretrial diversion. (*See* 18 U.S.C. § 1512, Historical and Statutory Notes, Federal Guidelines for Treatment of Crime Victims and Witnesses in the Criminal Justice System). Such conferences should be conducted consistent with applicable rules governing criminal procedure and professional conduct. Ordinarily, prosecutors should use such conferences to obtain relevant information from the victim and convey appropriate nonsensitive or public information to the victim. The conference provides victims the opportunity to express their views, keeping in mind that prosecution decisions are within the prosecutor's discretion. Department personnel should not provide legal advice to victims, either as part of these conferences or otherwise.

2. Proposed Plea Agreements

    Prosecutors should make reasonable efforts to notify identified victims of, and consider victims' views about, prospective plea negotiations. Prosecutors should make these reasonable efforts with a goal of providing victims with a meaningful opportunity to offer their views before a plea agreement is formally reached. In circumstances where plea negotiations occur before a case has been brought, Department policy is that this should include reasonable consultation prior to the filing of a charging instrument with the court. Such consultation may be general in nature and does not have to be specific to a particular plea offer or defendant but rather can be a wide solicitation of victim plea and sentencing views without reference to any particular defendant or person of interest. In determining whether and to what extent consultation is reasonable, the prosecutor should consider factors relevant to the propriety and practicality of giving notice and considering views in the context of the particular case, including, but not limited to, the following factors:

a. The impact on public safety and risks to personal safety.

b. The number of victims.

c. Whether time is of the essence in negotiating or entering a proposed plea.

d. Whether the proposed plea involves confidential information or conditions or whether some other need for confidentiality is present.

e. Whether the victim is a possible witness in the case and the effect that relaying any information may have on the defendant's right to a fair trial.

COMMENTARY

The reasonable right to confer concerning possible plea agreements does not obligate the prosecutor to consult with victims every time a term in the plea changes or when particular defendants are added or removed from an investigation or prosecution.

3. Cases With Large Numbers of Victims

In cases where the large number of victims makes individual consultation impractical, Department employees may nonetheless provide victims with information and seek their input through the use of alternative means such as Web sites, e-mails, conference calls, legal representatives, and town hall meetings.

H. Right to Full and Timely Restitution as Provided in Law

Victims have a right to "full and timely restitution as provided in law." (18 U.S.C. § 3771(a)(6)). Restitution is mandatory – regardless of the defendant's ability to pay – for most federal crimes. (*See* 18 U.S.C. § 3663A (2006)). Even when restitution is not mandatory, the sentencing court may require restitution in accordance with a plea agreement (18 U.S.C. § 3663A(a)(3)), or pursuant to the court's discretion. (18 U.S.C. § 3663 (2006 & Supp. II 2008)). In discretionary cases, the court may also require restitution as a condition of probation or supervised release.

All who investigate and prosecute criminal cases play an important role in determining whether restitution is full and timely. The scope of the victim's losses, the nexus between the victim's losses and the crimes charged, what happened to ill-gotten gains, and the defendant's ability to pay are all integral to the criminal prosecution. Restitution should be considered early in the investigation and throughout the prosecution. Prosecutors have a variety of tools to assure that ill-gotten gains are frozen or forfeited and later restored to victims of crime.

1. Focus on Restitution Early in the Investigation and Throughout the Case

    Actions taken at each stage of a case – from investigation, to charging, plea negotiations, and sentencing – all affect whether victims will receive full and timely restitution.

    a. Investigation

        Investigators should, to the extent reasonably practicable, identify victims and gather information on the extent of victims' losses, the nexus between those losses and the defendant's criminal conduct, and whether any assets exist that might be recovered, frozen, forfeited, or otherwise used to pay restitution.

    b. Charging

        The amount of restitution that a court may order is affected by the crimes charged. When exercising their discretion, prosecutors should give due consideration to the need to provide full restitution to the victims of federal criminal offenses.

    c. Prejudgment Restraint of Assets

        Defendants may dissipate or hide their ill-gotten gains as time passes. Prosecutors, during investigations, should consider freezing assets under 18 U.S.C. § 1345 (2006), or seizing assets for criminal or civil forfeiture. In cases where defendants are cooperative, prosecutors may also ask defendants for voluntary, signed agreements not to dissipate assets.

    d. Plea Discussions

        In plea negotiations, prosecutors should consider "requesting that the defendant provide full restitution to all victims of all charges contained in the indictment or information, without regard to the counts to which the defendant actually plead[s]." (USAM 9-16.320). When reasonably possible, plea agreements should identify victims' losses for purposes of restitution and address the manner of payment. Defendants who can pay some or all of the anticipated restitution should be asked to pay what they reasonably can by the time of sentencing. Under the Sentencing Guidelines, anticipatory payment of restitution is a factor in determining "acceptance of responsibility." (U.S.S.G. § 3E1.1, cmt. n.1(c)).

    e. Payments by Sentencing

        Defendants who have the ability to pay some or all of their restitution should be asked to pay what they reasonably can by the date of sentencing. (*See generally* 18 U.S.C. § 3572(d)(1) (2006)).

f. Presentence Investigation

Prosecutors and victim witness personnel should help assure that the probation office receives accurate information about victim names, addresses, and amounts subject to restitution. (*See* 18 U.S.C. § 3664(d)(1) (2006) "[T]he attorney for the government, after consulting, to the extent practicable, with all identified victims, shall promptly provide the probation officer with a listing of the amounts subject to restitution."). Additionally, if available, information should be provided to the probation office reflecting the defendant's ability to pay. The presentence report should contain, to the extent reasonably possible, accurate information about the defendant's financial condition. Prosecutors and their staff should review the presentence report for accuracy as to victim information and the defendant's ability to pay, and appropriate objections should be raised in a timely fashion.

g. Addressing Issues at Sentencing

Prosecutors and victim witness personnel should help assure that the court has accurate information about victim names, addresses, and loss amounts (inaccurate information may prevent the clerk of the court from disbursing restitution even when funds are available). Federal law provides that "[i]f the victim's losses are not ascertainable by the date that is 10 days prior to sentencing, the attorney for the Government or the probation officer shall so inform the court, and the court shall set a date for the final determination of the victim's loses, not to exceed 90 days after sentencing." (18 U.S.C. § 3664(d)(5)). In rare cases, restitution may not be ordered "if the court finds, from facts on the record, that – (A) the number of identifiable victims is so large as to make restitution impracticable; or (B) determining complex issues of fact related to the cause or amount of the victim's losses would complicate or prolong the sentencing process to a degree that the need to provide restitution to any victim is outweighed by the burden on the sentencing process." (18 U.S.C. § 3663A(c)(3)). In such cases, where forfeited assets are involved, prosecutors should consult with the Criminal Division's Asset Forfeiture and Money Laundering Section (AFMLS) to determine the most effective way of returning forfeited assets to victims. In cases with multiple defendants, the court should be asked to address joint and several liability. (18 U.S.C. § 3664(h)). Additionally, "[i]n any case in which the United States is a victim, the court shall ensure that all other victims receive full restitution before the United States receives any restitution." (18 U.S.C. § 3664(i)).

h. Orders of Restitution

To assure that restitution issues are addressed fully and accurately, prosecutors should consider tendering an order of restitution in conjunction with the sentencing. The order should identify all victims entitled to restitution, the amount of restitution for each victim, and, where appropriate, prioritization of payments among victims, methods, and schedules for payment, as well as issues of joint and several liability.

i. Payment Plans

By law, if a restitution order "permits other than immediate payment, the length of time over which scheduled payments will be made shall be set by the court, but shall be the shortest time in which full payment can reasonably be made." (18 U.S.C. § 3572(d)(2)). Payment plans should not be written or construed to prevent enforcement activity post judgment.

COMMENTARY

There are unique restitution issues in tax cases. When the United States seeks restitution in criminal tax cases, prosecutors should take care to avoid compromising the Internal Revenue Service's ability to collect the civil tax liability. In collecting restitution, prosecutors should be aware that there may be competing claims against the defendant's assets, including pre-existing tax liens, which may impact the actual amount available for restitution. Prosecutors should consult additional resources and the Tax Division regarding restitution in criminal tax cases and cases where defendants have tax liens.

2. Interplay Between Restitution and Asset Forfeiture

Whenever possible, prosecutors should use asset forfeiture to recover assets to return to victims of crime, as permitted by law. Government attorneys prosecuting civil or criminal forfeiture cases should assist crime victims in obtaining compensation in the following manner. If a defendant has sufficient assets to pay the restitution order without using property forfeitable to the government, the defendant must use those assets (not the forfeitable property) to satisfy the restitution order. If a defendant does not have sufficient assets to pay the restitution order without using forfeitable property, the government may use the procedural provisions of the forfeiture statutes to preserve and recover forfeitable property and to apply such property to the victims of the crime underlying the forfeiture.

There are essentially three methods by which the United States can use assets seized for forfeiture to compensate victims: direct transfers prior to forfeiture; requests for restoration of forfeited funds; and petitions for remission of forfeited funds. The first two methods are intended for use in conjunction with, and to assist in the satisfaction of, a restitution order entered in the criminal case. The third method is available in cases where no restitution order has been entered.

a. Forfeiture Proceedings Termination Before a Final Order of Forfeiture Is Entered

At the request of the United States, the district court may order that funds seized but not finally forfeited to the United States be paid to the clerk of the court toward the satisfaction of the defendant's restitution obligation. This option is particularly useful when the assets seized are liquid and when the victims are entitled to restitution for non-pecuniary losses such as physical or emotional injuries, or for other collateral costs that are not compensable under the remission regulations and there are no third-party claimants. (*See* Provisions Applicable to Victims, 28 C.F.R. § 9.8 (2010)).

b. Request for Restoration

The Restoration Policy set forth in Chapter 13, Section I.B of the *Asset Forfeiture Policy Manual* (2010) and Department of Justice Forfeiture Policy Directive 02-1– Guidelines and Procedures for Restoration of Forfeited Property to Crime Victims via Restitution in Lieu of Remission, allows AFMLS to restore criminally forfeited assets to victims of the offense underlying the forfeiture, who are named in a judicial restitution order, based on the losses recognized in a criminal restitution order. The prosecuting office submits the Request for Restoration on behalf of victims by certifying that the victims named in the court's restitution order meet the criteria for restoration under the policy. This option is particularly useful when multiple victims have incurred only economic losses, when the interest of third-party claimants must be determined, or when the forfeiture involves property that would be best liquidated by using asset forfeiture procedures.

c. Petition for Remission (Regulations Governing the Remission or Mitigation of Civil and Criminal Forfeitures, 28 C.F.R. pt. 9 (2010)).

Each individual victim can submit a Petition for Remission of judicially forfeited assets to the prosecuting office that obtains a report and recommendation from the seizing agency and then forwards the petition to AFMLS for a final determination. This option is particularly useful when there are victims of offenses that underlie civil forfeitures, but there is no companion criminal case or criminal proceedings terminated prior to conviction, and, thus, no order of restitution. This option is also useful where there is a criminal judgment and order of forfeiture, but the court has declined to issue an order of restitution, for example, where due to the complexity of the proceedings, entry of a restitution order in the criminal case would unduly prolong the underlying criminal proceedings. It is also useful in cases that involve only corporate entities.

3. Enforcement Post Sentencing

After judgments are entered, Financial Litigation Units should prioritize collection activity so that victims may receive full and timely restitution. Financial Litigation Units should investigate defendants' ability to pay, and should engage in vigorous enforcement methods, which may include filing liens, obtaining writs of execution or garnishment, or adding debtors to the Taxpayer Offset Program.

Victims shall receive timely notice of hearings involving enforcement activities. (18 U.S.C. § 3771(a)(2)).

Prosecutors should be mindful that defendants who knowingly refuse to pay may be resentenced. (18 U.S.C. § 3614(a) (2006)).

I. Right to Proceedings Free From Unreasonable Delay

A crime victim has the right to proceedings free from unreasonable delay. (18 U.S.C. § 3771(a)(7)).

Prosecutors should be reasonably available to consult with victims regarding significant adversities they may suffer as a result of delays in the prosecution of the case and should, at the appropriate time, inform the court of the reasonable concerns that have been conveyed to the prosecutor. Prosecutors should consider raising the victim's right to proceedings free from unreasonable delay when discussing trial dates and responding to defense motions for continuances. Prosecutors should also consider any victim adversities that may result from prosecution requests for continuances and make reasonable efforts to mitigate the delay where possible and consistent with the best interests of the prosecution.

J. Right to Fairness and Respect for Dignity and Privacy

A crime victim has the right to be treated with fairness and with respect for the victim's dignity and privacy. (18 U.S.C. § 3771(a)(8)).

1. Privacy

   Consistent with the purposes of 18 U.S.C. § 3771(a)(8), Department personnel engaged in the investigation or prosecution of a crime shall respect victims' privacy and employ best efforts to protect victims' personal information from unnecessary disclosure to the public. (*See* Article II.C.1.).

   Press inquiries and other attention from the media often implicate victim privacy concerns. Department personnel should refrain from providing public statements that identify or otherwise allude to the identity of the victim unless warranted for public safety reasons or other appropriate concerns.

2. Dignity

   Department personnel should likewise protect the dignity of victims, particularly those victims who have been exploited or are particularly vulnerable (e.g., children, developmentally challenged individuals, mentally ill individuals, or elderly persons). To the extent possible, Department personnel should inform and prepare victims for what evidence or potential testimony will be presented as well as what evidence may be revealed in proceedings. Prosecutors should aim to present material at trial or in hearings in such a manner that balances the presumption of public access to the courts with a victim's right to be treated with dignity. Motions *in limine*, protective orders, and other means should be used to prevent evidence impacting a victim's dignity from unnecessarily being viewed or disclosed in open court or otherwise revealed to the public at large, unless necessary for legitimate evidentiary purposes or to ensure compliance with court rules or rulings.

3. Fairness

Victims have the right to be treated with fairness. While the best interests of the government's case are of primary importance, when responding to motions, arguments, and requests for continuances, Department personnel should consider a victim's right to fairness when developing and presenting the government's position.

Barring legitimate law enforcement considerations, and when feasible under the particular circumstances of the case, Department personnel should use their best efforts to attempt to inform victims about significant public announcements concerning the investigation or prosecution of the case in advance of or concurrent with any Department efforts to inform the public or make a public statement.

K. In-Court Enforcement Mechanisms

Victims' rights under the CVRA may be enforced by motions filed by the government or the victim. (18 U.S.C. § 3771(d)(1); *see also* Fed. R. Crim. P. 60(b)(2)). Department prosecutors are encouraged to assert victims' rights when appropriate, taking into consideration the victim's preferences and the interests of the United States. Prosecutors are urged to analyze any potential issues related to victims' rights early in the case in order to be able to assert victims' rights at the first opportunity. When filing a motion in court, prosecutors should give consideration to victim privacy and take steps to prevent private information from unnecessary disclosure. When a victim files a motion that the Department does not support or that the prosecutor believes is not legally warranted, the government may oppose the motion or refrain from taking a position on the motion. In such circumstances, and whenever prosecutors have questions about enforcement mechanisms, personnel in the United States Attorneys' Offices are encouraged to consult with the Executive Office for United States Attorneys, and those in the litigating divisions are encouraged to consult with their responsible officials.

If the trial court denies a CVRA rights enforcement motion, the movant may petition the Court of Appeals for an expedited writ of mandamus that must issue within 72 hours. (18 U.S.C. § 3771(d)(3)). In addition, on direct appeal, the government may assert as error any denial of victims' rights in the proceeding to which the appeal relates. (18 U.S.C. § 3771(d)(4)). A government attorney seeking to file a petition for a writ of mandamus or a direct appeal must obtain written authorization from the Solicitor General, in addition to the approvals required by that attorney's office or section. *See* 28 C.F.R. § 0.20(b). To facilitate the authorization process, the attorney must prepare a written recommendation as to why appeal or mandamus is warranted in the case, and transmit that recommendation to the attorney's appellate section for them to prepare their own recommendation for the Solicitor General. In cases involving appeals or mandamus requests from divisions other than the Criminal Division, the attorney or the division's appellate section should consult with the Criminal Division's Appellate Section. Because the authorization process will generally extend beyond the time period for filing a valid notice of appeal, the attorney should file a protective notice of appeal within the applicable time period even though it has not yet been authorized. If the Solicitor General declines to authorize an appeal, the attorney must then file a motion to voluntarily dismiss the appeal.

[page intentionally left blank]

ARTICLE VI

WITNESSES

A. Victims' Services and Rights Laws Do Not Cover Witnesses

A person who has information or evidence concerning a crime, and provides information regarding his/her knowledge to a law enforcement agency, is a witness. Witnesses who do not fit the CVRA definition of crime victim do not have enforceable victims' rights, and the VRRA does not require Department personnel to provide witnesses with services. Department personnel should use reasonable efforts to do all that is possible within the limits of available resources, without infringing on the defendant's constitutional rights, to assist witnesses to crime during their interaction with the criminal justice system.

B. Witness Security

Department personnel should take reasonable measures to address the security concerns of witnesses. Determining the nature and scope of such measures requires an evaluation of the threat level and identification of reasonable options to address that threat within available resources. Witnesses have the choice whether to accept the reasonable options the Department offers.

The responsibility of arranging for reasonable witness security remains with the investigative agency throughout the criminal justice process. All Department personnel, however, should consider witness security concerns at every point in the criminal justice system and consult and coordinate with the investigative agency concerning witness security. Witness concerns about safety and reports of threats should immediately be reported to the lead case agent.

Department personnel should use their discretion and sound judgment when discussing possible threats andsecurity measures with witnesses. Trained personnel should make witnesses aware of the resources that maybe available to promote their safety.

Responsible officials from the investigation, prosecution, and corrections components, as well as the Parole Commission, are encouraged to work together to meet safety concerns. United States Attorneys are encouraged to work with responsible officials from investigative agencies to develop collaborative procedures to meet witness safety concerns in their districts.

Admission into the Federal Witness Security Program is an extreme measure that is only available to crucial witnesses in significant prosecutions who are in life-threatening danger. Admission to the Program must be sponsored by a prosecutor and the final determination of Program availability is made by designated officials in the Criminal Division's Office of Enforcement Operations (OEO). Responsible officials in law enforcement agencies and prosecutor's offices are not authorized to promise witnesses Program admission nor can witnesses rely on such promises absent approval by appropriate OEO officials.

C. Logistical Assistance

Prosecution agencies are responsible for informing and assisting witnesses with information about transportation, parking, childcare, translator services, and other logistical matters in connection with court appearances and witness conferences. The Parole Commission is responsible for informing and assisting witnesses with similar services in connection with parole hearings.

D. Notification of Offender Release

Department personnel may include witnesses in offender release notifications if the situation warrants.

ARTICLE VII

NON-LITIGABILITY

The AG Guidelines are intended to provide internal Department guidance for the treatment of victims of and witnesses to crime, recognizing that the circumstances presented by each case cannot be adequately predicted in advance. Consequently, decisions regarding the treatment of victims of and witnesses to crime frequently will require assessments, evaluations, and the exercise of independent judgment in light of the circumstances presented. The AG Guidelines are not intended to, do not, and should not be relied upon to create any procedural or substantive rights or to establish procedural or substantive standards of conduct or care enforceable at law in any matter, civil or criminal. No limitations are hereby intended or placed on otherwise lawful prerogatives of the Department.

[page intentionally left blank]

APPENDIX A

VICTIMS' RIGHTS AND RESTITUTION ACT (VRRA), 42 U.S.C. § 10607 (2006)

42 U.S.C § 10607

(a) Designation of responsible officials

The head of each department and agency of the United States engaged in the detection, investigation, or prosecution of crime shall designate by names and office titles the persons who will be responsible for identifying the victims of crime and performing the services described in subsection (c) of this section at each stage of a criminal case.

(b) Identification of victims

At the earliest opportunity after the detection of a crime at which it may be done without interfering with an investigation, a responsible official shall –

(1) identify the victim or victims of a crime;

(2) inform the victims of their right to receive, on request, the services described in subsection (c) of this section; and

(3) inform each victim of the name, title, and business address and telephone number of the responsible official to whom the victim should address a request for each of the services described in subsection (c) of this section.

(c) Description of services

(1) A responsible official shall –

(A) inform a victim of the place where the victim may receive emergency medical and social services;

(B) inform a victim of any restitution or other relief to which the victim may be entitled under this or any other law and manner in which such relief may be obtained;

(C) inform a victim of public and private programs that are available to provide counseling, treatment, and other support to the victim; and

(D) assist a victim in contacting the persons who are responsible for providing the services and relief described in subparagraphs (A), (B), and (C).

(2) A responsible official shall arrange for a victim to receive reasonable protection from a suspected offender and persons acting in concert with or at the behest of the suspected offender.

(3) During the investigation and prosecution of a crime, a responsible official shall provide a victim the earliest possible notice of –

    (A) the status of the investigation of the crime, to the extent it is appropriate to inform the victim and to the extent that it will not interfere with the investigation;

    (B) the arrest of a suspected offender;

    (C) the filing of charges against a suspected offender;

    (D) the scheduling of each court proceeding that the witness is either required to attend or, under section 10606(b)(4) of this title, is entitled to attend;

    (E) the release or detention status of an offender or suspected offender;

    (F) the acceptance of a plea of guilty or nolo contendere or the rendering of a verdict after trial; and

    (G) the sentence imposed on an offender, including the date on which the offender will be eligible for parole.

(4) During court proceedings, a responsible official shall ensure that a victim is provided a waiting area removed from and out of the sight and hearing of the defendant and defense witnesses.

(5) After trial, a responsible official shall provide a victim the earliest possible notice of –

    (A) the scheduling of a parole hearing for the offender;

    (B) the escape, work release, furlough, or any other form of release from custody of the offender; and

    (C) the death of the offender, if the offender dies while in custody.

(6) At all times, a responsible official shall ensure that any property of a victim that is being held for evidentiary purposes be maintained in good condition and returned to the victim as soon as it is no longer needed for evidentiary purposes.

(7) The Attorney General or the head of another department or agency that conducts an investigation of a sexual assault shall pay, either directly or by reimbursement of payment by the victim, the cost of a physical examination of the victim which an investigating officer determines was necessary or useful for evidentiary purposes. The Attorney General shall provide for the payment of the cost of up to 2 anonymous and confidential tests of the victim for sexually transmitted diseases, including HIV, gonorrhea, herpes, chlamydia, and syphilis, during the 12 months following sexual assaults that pose a risk of transmission, and the cost of a counseling session by a

medically trained professional on the accuracy of such tests and the risk of transmission of sexually transmitted diseases to the victim as the result of the assault. A victim may waive anonymity and confidentiality of any tests paid for under this section.

(8) A responsible official shall provide the victim with general information regarding the corrections process, including information about work release, furlough, probation, and eligibility for each.

(d) No cause of action or defense

This section does not create a cause of action or defense in favor of any person arising out of the failure of a responsible person to provide information as required by subsection (b) or (c) of this section.

(e) Definitions

For the purposes of this section –

(1) the term "responsible official" means a person designated pursuant to subsection (a) of this section to perform the functions of a responsible official under that section; and

(2) the term "victim" means a person that has suffered direct physical, emotional, or pecuniary harm as a result of the commission of a crime, including –

    (A) in the case of a victim that is an institutional entity, an authorized representative of the entity; and

    (B) in the case of a victim who is under 18 years of age, incompetent, incapacitated, or deceased, one of the following (in order of preference):

        (i) a spouse;

        (ii) a legal guardian;

        (iii) a parent;

        (iv) a child;

        (v) a sibling;

        (vi) another family member; or

        (vii) another person designated by the court.

[page intentionally left blank]

APPENDIX B

CRIME VICTIMS' RIGHTS ACT (CVRA), 18 U.S.C. § 3771 (2006 & SUPP. III 2009)

18 U.S.C. § 3771

(a) Rights of crime victims – A crime victim has the following rights:

   (1) The right to be reasonably protected from the accused.

   (2) The right to reasonable, accurate, and timely notice of any public court proceeding, or any parole proceeding, involving the crime or of any release or escape of the accused.

   (3) The right not to be excluded from any such public court proceeding, unless the court, after receiving clear and convincing evidence, determines that testimony by the victim would be materially altered if the victim heard other testimony at that proceeding.

   (4) The right to be reasonably heard at any public proceeding in the district court involving release, plea, sentencing, or any parole proceeding.

   (5) The reasonable right to confer with the attorney for the Government in the case.

   (6) The right to full and timely restitution as provided in law.

   (7) The right to proceedings free from unreasonable delay.

   (8) The right to be treated with fairness and with respect for the victim's dignity and privacy.

(b) Rights afforded. –

   (1) In general. – In any court proceeding involving an offense against a crime victim, the court shall ensure that the crime victim is afforded the rights described in subsection (a). Before making a determination described in subsection (a)(3), the court shall make every effort to permit the fullest attendance possible by the victim and shall consider reasonable alternatives to the exclusion of the victim from the criminal proceeding. The reasons for any decision denying relief under this chapter shall be clearly stated on the record.

   (2) Habeas corpus proceedings. –

      (A) In general. – In a Federal habeas corpus proceeding arising out of a State conviction, the court shall ensure that a crime victim is afforded the rights described in paragraphs (3), (4), (7), and (8) of subsection (a).

(B) Enforcement. –

   (i) In general. – These rights may be enforced by the crime victim or the crime victim's lawful representative in the manner described in paragraphs (1) and (3) of subsection (d).

   (ii) Multiple victims. – In a case involving multiple victims, subsection (d)(2) shall also apply.

(C) Limitation. – This paragraph relates to the duties of a court in relation to the rights of a crime victim in Federal habeas corpus proceedings arising out of a State conviction, and does not give rise to any obligation or requirement applicable to personnel of any agency of the Executive Branch of the Federal Government.

(D) Definition – For purposes of this paragraph, the term "crime victim" means the person against whom the State offense is committed or, if that person is killed or incapacitated, that person's family member or other lawful representative.

(c) Best efforts to accord rights –

   (1) Government. – Officers and employees of the Department of Justice and other departments and agencies of the United States engaged in the detection, investigation, or prosecution of crime shall make their best efforts to see that crime victims are notified of, and accorded, the rights described in subsection (a).

   (2) Advice of attorney. – The prosecutor shall advise the crime victim that the crime victim can seek the advice of an attorney with respect to the rights described in subsection (a).

   (3) Notice. – Notice of release otherwise required pursuant to this chapter shall not be given if such notice may endanger the safety of any person.

(d) Enforcement and limitations. –

   (1) Rights. – The crime victim or the crime victim's lawful representative, and the attorney for the Government may assert the rights described in subsection (a). A person accused of the crime may not obtain any form of relief under this chapter.

   (2) Multiple crime victims. – In a case where the court finds that the number of crime victims makes it impracticable to accord all of the crime victims the rights described in subsection (a), the court shall fashion a reasonable procedure to give effect to this chapter that does not unduly complicate or prolong the proceedings.

   (3) Motion for relief and writ of mandamus. – The rights described in subsection (a) shall be asserted in the district court in which a defendant is being prosecuted for the crime or, if no prosecution is underway, in the district court in the district in

which the crime occurred. The district court shall take up and decide any motion asserting a victim's right forthwith. If the district court denies the relief sought, the movant may petition the court of appeals for a writ of mandamus. The court of appeals may issue the writ on the order of a single judge pursuant to circuit rule or the Federal Rules of Appellate Procedure. The court of appeals shall take up and decide such application forthwith within 72 hours after the petition has been filed. In no event shall proceedings be stayed or subject to a continuance of more than five days for purposes of enforcing this chapter. If the court of appeals denies the relief sought, the reasons for the denial shall be clearly stated on the record in a written opinion.

(4) Error. – In any appeal in a criminal case, the Government may assert as error the district court's denial of any crime victim's right in the proceeding to which the appeal relates.

(5) Limitation on relief. – In no case shall a failure to afford a right under this chapter provide grounds for a new trial. A victim may make a motion to re-open a plea or sentence only if –

(A) the victim has asserted the right to be heard before or during the proceeding at issue and such right was denied;

(B) the victim petitions the court of appeals for a writ of mandamus within 14 days; and

(C) in the case of a plea, the accused has not pled to the highest offense charged.

This paragraph does not affect the victim's right to restitution as provided in title 18, United States Code.

(6) No cause of action. – Nothing in this chapter shall be construed to authorize a cause of action for damages or to create, to enlarge, or to imply any duty or obligation to any victim or other person for the breach of which the United States or any of its officers or employees could be held liable in damages. Nothing in this chapter shall be construed to impair the prosecutorial discretion of the Attorney General or any officer under his direction.

(e) Definitions. – For the purposes of this chapter, the term "crime victim" means a person directly and proximately harmed as a result of the commission of a Federal offense or an offense in the District of Columbia. In the case of a crime victim who is under 18 years of age, incompetent, incapacitated, or deceased, the legal guardians of the crime victim or the representatives of the crime victim's estate, family members, or any other persons appointed as suitable by the court, may assume the crime victim's rights under this chapter, but in no event shall the defendant be named as such guardian or representative.

(f) Procedures to promote compliance. –

    (1) Regulations. – Not later than 1 year after the date of enactment of this chapter, the Attorney General of the United States shall promulgate regulations to enforce the rights of crime victims and to ensure compliance by responsible officials with the obligations described in law respecting crime victims.

    (2) Contents. – The regulations promulgated under paragraph (1) shall –

        (A) designate an administrative authority within the Department of Justice to receive and investigate complaints relating to the provision or violation of the rights of a crime victim;

        (B) require a course of training for employees and offices of the Department of Justice that fail to comply with provisions of Federal law pertaining to the treatment of crime victims, and otherwise assist such employees and offices in responding more effectively to the needs of crime victims;

        (C) contain disciplinary sanctions, including suspension or termination from employment, for employees of the Department of Justice who willfully or wantonly fail to comply with provisions of Federal law pertaining to the treatment of crime victims; and

        (D) provide that the Attorney General, or the designee of the Attorney General, shall be the final arbiter of the complaint, and that there shall be no judicial review of the final decision of the Attorney General by a complainant.

www.ingramcontent.com/pod-product-compliance
Lightning Source LLC
Chambersburg PA
CBHW081605170526
15166CB00009B/2035